CH00693634

THE CRY
of the
SHEPHERD
THE LION HAS ROARED

Y. M. TIKKUN

The Cry of the Shepherd © Copyright 2019 by Y.M. Tikkun

All rights reserved. This book is protected by the copyright laws of the United States of America. No part of this publication may be reproduced, stored in a retrieval system, or transmitted in any form or by any means— electronic, mechanical, photocopy, recording, or any other— except for brief quotations in printed reviews, without permission in writing from the publisher and/or the author.

Publisher's Cataloging-In-Publication Data
(Prepared by The Donohue Group, Inc.)

Names: Tikkun, Y. M., author.
Title: *The cry of the Shepherd : the Lion has roared* / Y.M. Tikkun.
Description: Cleveland, TN : Deeper Revelation Books, [2019] |
    Series: [Shepherd trilogy] ; [3]
Identifiers: ISBN 9781949297089
Subjects: LCSH: Private revelations. | Spiritual life--Christianity. | Jesus Christ--Words.
Classification: LCC BV5091.R4 T553 2019 | DDC 248.29--dc23

ARTWORK
The front cover art of this book was created by Barbara Leone.
Interior illustrations are by Ainsley Bennett.
The lamb/lion illustration on the back cover and the graphic layout of the book are by Jeff Johnson.

CAPITALIZATION NOTE
Please note that certain pronouns referring to God in Scripture have been capitalized, even if that is not the case in the original. We have chosen to do this in honor to the Creator. Also, the name satan and related names or titles are not capitalized. We choose not to acknowledge him even to the point of violating grammatical rules.

Published by Deeper Revelation Books
Revealing "the deep things of God" (1 Cor. 2:10)
P.O. Box 4260
Cleveland, TN, USA 37320-4260
Phone: 423-478-2843
Email: info@deeperrevelationbooks.org
Website: www.deeperrevelationbooks.org

Deeper Revelation Books assists Christian authors in publishing and distributing their books. Final responsibility for design, content, permissions, editorial accuracy, and doctrinal views, either expressed or implied, belongs to the author.

CKNOWLEDGMENTS

In a season of upheaval and war, it is vital that we hear the voice of our Divine Shepherd. To be effective followers, we first must be effective and attentive listeners. He has already told us that His true sheep hear His voice, and they recognize it, even amid the clamor of many other voices. When His truth goes forth, His attentive, obedient lambs follow with a heart of trusting love, wherever He leads.

This humble scribe has been gifted, since childhood, to hear the precious voice of our beloved Shepherd. To always be available, to come away, to record whatever gems of wisdom the Shepherd wants to impart to His flock, can be a challenge in a busy life. Scribes in the kingdom must be blessed with loved ones who have the grace and the vision to set them free to attend to that work. I have been blessed with a spouse who loves the Shepherd as dearly as I do. He has the revelation regarding the veracity of this gifting, as well as the vital nature of this scribe's work. He freed me to write, while he alone carried the responsibility of providing the income for our family. I praise YHVH for the amazing blessing that I have been given in this marriage to my beloved Doug. While so many spouses demand primary time and attention, many times Doug has blessed me to attend to the Shepherd's call, rather than attending to his personal needs or desires. Thank you, darling!

I have also been blessed to have a steadfast and gifted sister in the Lord who brought forth the wonderful cover art for this book. It was birthed in the Spirit after many hours of seeking

His guidance through prayer. This beautiful book cover is truly a labor of great love. Thank you, Barbara!

So many encouraging sisters and brothers in the Lord, throughout the world, have prayed for this third book in the Shepherd trilogy to come into publication. They have affirmed my ability to hear the Shepherd and blessed me with countless reports of how His words, recorded in these books, have enriched their lives. Thank you so much!

I also would like to acknowledge the faith, care, wisdom, and heart of the staff at Deeper Revelation Books in bringing this inspired manuscript into print. Mike Shreve, Vickie, and the rest of the team at Deeper Revelation Books have a heart for excellence and a love for the Kingdom that serves the Shepherd very well. They, too, hear and recognize His voice— following it wherever He leads. I bless you, Mike and staff! Thank you for holding this material so carefully, and for producing it so excellently.

Above all else, I bless and honor the One who has enabled me to serve as His scribe in these writings. I pray that the great Shepherd will always find me faithful to His call. My heart is to hear and to obey, whether to sit before Him with pen in hand, or to rise up for the sake of His flock and Kingdom, when His cry goes forth ... calling me to battle at His side.

TABLE OF CONTENTS

ADDITIONAL RESOURCES

PROTOCOLS FOR PRAYER WARRIORS

OREWORD

"I have called you to be in total submission to My leadership, following Me wherever I lead, but I have wanted more from you than convenient, self-sustaining obedience. My heart is to position you for victory in every battle. Every victory is enabled by the sacrificial obedience that arises only from a surrendered heart of deep love and devotion. Surely, I have the power to control you, but, because of My covenant at the beginning of time, I have set you free to choose Me or to choose your own way. That makes me a unique Shepherd and gives you the possibility of being an extraordinary sheep."
(Excerpt from Chapter 17, "Unity and Mutiny")

As with the first two volumes in the Shepherd series, *The Cry of the Shepherd* was given into my spirit as I sojourned in Jerusalem, Israel. Perpetually, there is something about this city that is extraordinary, even as she struggles to claim her place in the world and to demonstrate her prophesied fulfillment as written in the Bible's scriptures. Given that this city was established as His own possession by the mouth of the Creator and designated as the capital of the Messiah's Kingdom on earth, it's not surprising that it's the central location on the planet for the highest level of spiritual warfare.

It is no wonder that I was sent here to receive instruction concerning the rules, the orders, and the strategies for victory in the battle between good and evil. Keep in mind, however, that the great Shepherd has already defeated the ultimate enemy. The war that rages now, and which will rage until the end of time, is one fought between the enemy and the sheep … i.e., the human children of YHVH. This is not a war that any of us can avoid, no matter how hard we try.

This writing, while given by the same Spirit as the two previous Shepherd volumes, has a greater intensity than either of them. *The Whispers of the Shepherd* was presented as the conception of a new love. It flowed from the Spirit into my thoughts and onto the pages like a divine embrace: enwrapping one who is dearly loved. While The Whispers came forth in gentle quietness, *The Call of the Shepherd* was a labor requiring sharp focus and concentrated perseverance to move the inspired messages onto the pages. The second volume was the growth phase of that which was conceived in the first. It spoke of maturity that would require hard work and deliberate effort to take us from being mere carnal beings into the ripeness of the Spirit. Where *The Call of the Shepherd* ends, *The Cry of the Shepherd* begins. As the first two books were about conception and maturity, this one is about birthing Kingdom warriors who will be battle ready.

The Cry of the Shepherd was born out of the Spirit in great effort, which, at times, included the agony of my soul. Waves of powerful revelation would come, often accompanied by resistance from the opposing forces that did not want this birth to be accomplished as written pages to be shared. Distractions and challenges rose up day and night in an attempt to discourage me, so that I would lay down the assignment. Without explanation, hours of typing would suddenly disappear from the computer screen, if I left it momentarily to take a break. By God's grace alone, I have been able to persevere.

Even as I type these words, a physical example of these challenges is resounding in my ears. The very day that I began to write down the inspirations coming into my spirit, the apartment adjacent to mine began major renovations. Jack hammers, sledge hammers, and stone drills reverberated all around me. The walls of my apartment shook with the violence going on next door. My eardrums were assaulted with deafening noise to the point that it was impossible to carry on a phone conversation. Day after day, hour after hour, the apartment just beyond my walls was being totally taken apart and gutted. Walls came crashing down. Windows were forced out of their frames sending glass shattering to the stone floors. Yes, stone floors! The walls and floors of homes in Jerusalem are made of stone. They are profoundly resistant to being dismantled or moved. They conduct sound very well from one dwelling to another. Even during the time of Shabbat, when all work next door had ceased, there would be a consistent banging, as a partially disconnected door would whack against a wall as it was blown by the wind. Throughout the whole process, there would be occasional outbursts of loud, verbal confrontation as the workers and the foreman would challenge each other.

I cried out to the Shepherd asking why this was happening now, when it was so important for me to hear and record His messages? His response was that the day of battle, which was about to begin, would be very noisy, filled with "surround sound" chaos. The enemy would be vicious and violent in his opposition to the Shepherd's advancing Kingdom. It would be vital for the servants of the Shepherd to hear His voice amid the surrounding clamor of war. Trained, focused listening would be an urgent skill to have in the days to come. Additionally, the Shepherd wanted to prove, to me, His capability of making His voice heard clearly by those who would focus upon it and who would attend to His cry. His passionate war cry, and His orders within the battles, will carry us to victory, but we must be able to hear what He is saying in the thick of overwhelming clamor and challenge.

There may be a high cost to us, personally, as we stretch out, making it our priority to hear Him, but the cost will be well worth the benefit. We WILL hear Him. Then, as we follow Him, we will have strength in the fight, shalom in the struggles, and victory at the end of the war.

11

As if the physical challenges, accompanying the construction next door in Jerusalem, were not enough I was presented with challenges within my own soul. In the midst of writing, I was asked to deal with conflicts of personalities and priorities being raised with, and between, some people I love. In the midst of writing, a friend would phone to report a crisis that needed immediate counsel, intervention, or prayer. With each need that arose, I sought the counsel of the Shepherd to help me know how to respond. Should I leave the writing to address the urgent need presented to me, or should I attend to this manuscript? The decision would have to come from His Spirit, not from my soul, or from the demands of another person's soul. Time and time again, He would grant me the grace to fulfill His purposes in each challenge. Many times, when the challenge of soul was upon me, The Shepherd's direction would come in the form of one of the chapters in this book. He would suddenly drop His words into my heart as I sat attentively before Him: exposing the problem and revealing the solution. Clarity, strength, priority, and wisdom would come to lead me away from the inclinations of my flesh in order to apprehend His way of dealing with these things. Rather than being distractions, these situations were delivered to me as examples of ways that the enemy tries to bring defeat into the flock. Disunity and self-will showed themselves to be the hazards addressed in the chapter, "Unity and Mutiny." The chapter titled "A Way Through the Wilderness" birthed a sharp clarity in understanding as I cried out to the Shepherd on behalf of those experiencing the dry desert days of their journey with Him … days which would, eventually, refine them as gold. Chapter after chapter, the weight of demands on my time and focus continued. The noise surrounded me, but an increasing focus and strength grew within me. The pressure and the pain surrounding me were moving the Cry forward … out of the Spirit and down into the world.

Looking back upon the noise and distress surrounding me as this book was being born, I can see the Master's hand at work. He was blessing me in the midst of it all. Birth requires us to let go of our own inclinations in order to yield to the powerful forces established by our great Shepherd, so that He can bring about what He longs to see born upon the earth. That is the message I believe that He wanted me to experience deeply and personally as this manuscript was being written. The purpose of conception and maturing is to bring into being the potential and purpose that is already within us, so that we can stand upon the earth in victorious strength. What He has conceived in us for these coming days of battle must be matured, but then it must be delivered in the way, in the timing, and in the form, which He has ordained. If we have a flawed conception, based upon falsehoods out of the dark world or out of the turmoil of our own soul, the potential life intended for us to deliver will be naturally aborted. If we refuse the process He brings to break our flesh, and if we reject the time required for us to mature, we will not survive well in the world situations unfolding before us. If we are unwilling to submit to the helplessness and violence innate to birthing … if we are unwilling to trust in His hand to deliver us … we will never walk in the strength that comes from being born of His character.

The Cry of the Shepherd is much like the strong contractions that impose themselves upon our comfort. They squeeze us into tight places, taking away our power to resist. Our desire may be to stay where we are, but we will eventually face the reality that the world around us is changing in ways that will make it impossible for us to stay there. Our only recourse is to submit and to accept the breaking of the secure membranes, which, up to now, have provided us with a secure place to abide. It's time to allow Him to move us from where we have been, and from what we have understood, into new territory. It is time for us to move from our own independence and self-will into the ranks of a holy army comprised of bond servant sheep. There is no going back. The spiritual war is raging. Our Shepherd is shouting a cry for us to engage in the battle for His Kingdom.

In practical specifics, what does this mean? The members of the flock must come into His training program and into His understanding of the ways of spiritual war. For too long, the enemy has been able to take advantage of our weaknesses, double-mindedness, and ignorance. For too long, our souls have been inspired by our own personal, religious, agendas, under the guise of being godly and in order. Our war against darkness is about to intensify greatly. It's time for us to come under our Shepherd's total command and to lay aside our territorial claims, our demands for position, and our personal agendas. It is time for us to come into unity and to use our maturity to benefit His Kingdom.

Unknowingly, we have all been used as pawns by the enemy at times. Casually, we have ignored the sounds of battle, or drowned them out by indulging ourselves in distractions. Sometimes, we have turned to face the battle and found ourselves at war with our own egos or with our sense of personal competence. Sometimes, taking too much upon ourselves, we have become overwhelmed and fearful— leaving the ranks of the army to hide away. Too often, we have been consumed with battling each other while the enemy was busy claiming ground that we neglected to defend, liberate, or capture. Often, we have let down our guard following a victory. We've laid aside our weapons and abandoned our warrior focus to go on with our personal, civilian, life. We got all caught up in the party of a victory dance— believing that the war had ended. We changed into our "play" clothes and stopped listening for the voice of the Shepherd King. In doing so, we ignored the war and tuned out the cry to battle while the Enemy advanced. Then, when the losses began to move across our lives in waves, we blamed others, or we blamed the Shepherd. Whenever we replace The Shepherd as our priority, and whenever we decide to call the shots … and to interpret the events of life from our own grid of soul … we show contempt for the leadership of our Shepherd. In those times, we have allowed the plans of the Enemy to prosper. Even worse, in disregard for the Shepherd's sovereign authority, sometimes we have spoken arrogantly and acted rebelliously against His commands. We have acted treasonously.

The Cry of the Shepherd is a call to arms. First, we are to come into His loving embrace: giving to Him all that we are and all that we seek to accomplish for ourselves. In that moment, we also must choose to submit to His leadership in all matters. Then, we are to lay down our offenses and the weapons we have employed against each other. As we submit to His leadership, correction, and teaching, we will clearly see the true enemy ... the opposing force in our struggle for truth and righteousness. We must wake up to the realities of the war and to the role we must play. Finally, we must pick up the weapons of war that the Shepherd has ordained for us. Too often, we want to choose our own regiment or squadron, and the armaments that are most comfortable to us. He, however, often selects surprise, "out-of-the-box" assignments for us ... ones for which we will need to be trained and equipped. He will give us assignments for which we will be totally unprepared and totally unsuccessful without His commands leading us and without our retooling and training. Any victory will be accomplished through Him alone. We have broken ranks too often. We have turned to battle each other, totally ignoring the enemy breaking through our lines and ravaging our camps. We have left our Shepherd's training program prematurely, feeling that we already passed the course and already understood what needed to be done. Our understanding and our skills are incomplete. Some of us have been discontented with being foot soldiers and have pushed our way into a more prestigious leadership role, which was not ordained for us (and for which we are not suited). The result of this disorder has been evidenced in the Shepherd's army marching in competitive circles, while the enemy is moving forward in rank and in power. All that must stop.

If the Shepherd has already accomplished the victory for us, why are we struggling so much in this war? The Shepherd accomplished total victory over death and hell. But, being

15

creations of free will, we are allowed to choose the Kingdom we will serve … and whether we will claim the achieved victory and live in it. This is a battle for human souls. This is a battle for truth and righteousness. There truly is a war going on between good and evil, with the prize being the souls and societies of all human beings. Maybe we have been too distracted to notice the war. Maybe we have denied its reality. Maybe we have been so full of our own lives that we have neglected to appropriate His life for us. Our wisdom has been lacking. Our discernment has been weak. Our hearts have been divided. We have been playing with unholy fire. Pride has motivated our thought processes and our course of action. Often our strength has been drawn from sources other than from Him. All that must change.

If this book can raise up even a portion of His flock to successfully understand and engage in the warfare, it will have been worth every minute of labor that was required to birth it. Certainly, receiving these words, and recording them to be shared on these pages, has changed me: giving me a profound blessing. The connection between the demolition next door and the delivery of this book did not escape my notice. As the old was being demolished just beyond my apartment walls, the Lord was taking sledge hammers to wrongful patterns, assumptions, and priorities of soul that have held credible influence in the "flock" for a long time … even in me. Once started, the process must continue on to completion. Just as traditional labor in childbirth, once it begins, it must continue until the child is born into the world, in the same way, once *The Cry of the Shepherd* has gone forth, it, too, must continue to press us onward until the war between us and the enemy is over. I pray that we all will hear our loving Shepherd's commanding cry for us to come up for war, as the tribes of Israel were once called forth in a time of battle against enemies. Only by assuming our positions, and by operating under His authority/strategies, can we accomplish His victory: utterly humiliating our Enemy. There are multitudes of captives to be set free, and much ground to be taken back from the enemy. In the process of serving as a warrior in His army, we will achieve a deeper freedom, and a greater intimacy, with the One, who leads us onward. Hear His cry: "Arise, flock! To war! To victory!"

"*Al tirah!*" ... fear not! For the Shepherd leads us with absolute sovereignty, with perfect wisdom, and with absolute love.

"For the LORD of hosts has visited His flock,
the house of Judah,
And will make them like His majestic horse
in battle."
"From them will come the cornerstone,
From them the tent peg,
From them the bow of battle,
From them every ruler, all of them together."
"They will be as mighty men,
Treading down the enemy in the mire
of the streets in battle;
And they will fight, for the LORD will be with them;
And the riders on horses will be put to shame"
Zechariah 10: 3b-5 (NASB).

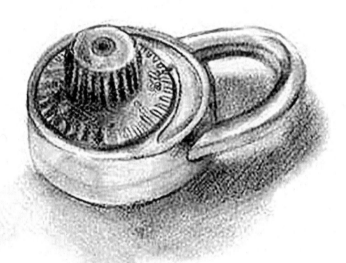

LOCK DOWN

Precious little ones, can you feel the unholy swirl of evil, as it organizes the great whirlwind of destruction? The spiral is yet too wide and too slow in its movement for the undiscerning to sense it. But to you, my faithful ones, to you, I have sent the awareness of its arising, and of its formation. Unholy winds are gathering. They are picking up momentum. The sounds of these winds are still too low for most to perceive them, and, yet, they continue to blow and to move across the world. They are already picking up people to carry them along, even as they are picking up momentum. Soon they will pick up institutions and cities, governments and even nations. Who is mindful of these things? Who perceives these developing portents of things to come? And how soon will they come upon you in manifestations of the obvious for all to see?

Little ones, what is your response to the revelation of these developments of which I now speak to you? How should you respond to these things? LOCK DOWN, I say.

LOCK DOWN those things that are called to endure through the coming storm. Those things, which now flap and fly about loosely in the beginning breezes, will soon be torn to bits in the blasts to come. All that is insecure will be tossed, inverted, and crushed by the weight of the falling atmospheric pressure of the spiritual storm.

LOCK DOWN those things within you, which are prone to shifting about in the midst of storming.

LOCK DOWN the treasures that I have given to you. Deposit them securely within the deep inner storehouses of safety at the center of your spirit.

LOCK DOWN your wandering thoughts and speculations. Focus, and focus yet again, on My word and upon My voice.

LOCK DOWN also your resolve to be steadfast. Secure tightly the calling I have placed within you by committing it to your will as well as to Mine.

LOCK DOWN your emotions that tend to fly about in reaction to adversity or challenge. Fear will be as a great sail in the winds of adversity, which if unfurled will serve to transport you off course and into the reefs of great destruction.

LOCK DOWN your free-floating appetites of soul. Give up your desire to be vindicated by your own efforts of self-justification. Surrender up your need to be right, acknowledged, and affirmed. Crucify your need to be comfortable and to be satiated by the things of the world and by the opinions of men. Put aside all self-indulgence. Let your hunger be for Me alone and for all that I desire of you and for you.

LOCK DOWN your need to know everything, tethering this need firmly to the reality of My eternal truth, the fullness of which is beyond your understanding. The enlightenment of the human mind will be the first casualty of the storm, as the perceived wisdom of men will be proven utterly false.

LOCK DOWN the fleeting minutes of your life, as you place each one under the authority of My eternal timetable. Put aside both your calendar and your clock. Listen for the beat of My heart and, also, for the sound of My alarm. Let Me own and direct your hours and your days, so that, in the roar of the storm, there shall be no panic in the passing days. My timing is perfect. All shall be accomplished according to my plan, not according to the intention of the storm. According to the sound of My voice the storm shall cease and never return.

All that can be moved off course … all that can be shaken … will soon succumb to the blast of unholy winds, directed by My hand, yet not created by My hand. It serves Me to bring these winds forth from behind the walls of My restraining power. Your safety will be in Me. LOCK DOWN in Me all that you are and all that you would hope to be. LOCK DOWN and attach yourself firmly to the Rock which is your shelter and your salvation. Use these days to help LOCK DOWN all those whom you love as well. If they will not hear or see the advancing storm, place each one within the shelter of My hand. I have ways unknown to you which will bring them to awareness and to security in Me. The day of the Lord approaches. Behold, it is closely at hand. LOCK DOWN and STAND! The storm of evil shall be reversed and destroyed by My decree and by the breath of My power. Until that glorious day, LOCK DOWN, little ones, and stand upon Me.

A WAY THROUGH
THE WILDERNESS

You are on a journey, little ones. Sometimes that journey will be easy … abundant in delightful food, flowing with cool water. At other times the road may be easy, but rather colorless, with fewer of the pleasures and comforts you would enjoy. Still other times, you will find yourself in the midst of a wilderness. Supply may be hidden … the path will be rocky or full of thorns … your map will not fit the location … and you are filled with anxiety. Where should you turn? How do you survive? Why are you here? Has your soul ever been consumed with these questions?

Wildernesses are an important part of your growth and training. I will bring them into your experience deliberately. You, at any time, of your own accord, may turn away from My assigned route for you, and, thereby, take yourself into the wilderness as well. I will allow it for your learning. Know this: even as a wilderness has a way out, it also has a purpose to be served. Give yourself to the learning, and I will show you the way out. If you focus the energy of your soul on escaping the wilderness, you will tire quickly and find yourself in the wilderness longer. If you stretch out in the Spirit and attend to what you are to see, hear, and glean from the wilderness, your exit will certainly be accomplished more quickly. Your time in the wilderness may even become cherished days, if you allow Me to walk through the challenges with you. Would you be surprised if you were hesitant to leave the wilderness, once you arrived at its exit, because of the sweet fellowship we two will have enjoyed in the midst of it? This, also, may become your experience.

What does the wilderness look like to your perceptions, little ones? The most immediate impression of this environment will be that you are ALONE. It is as if the wilderness absorbs all those fellows around you, making them invisible. At one time the whole nation of My people was subjected to many years in the wilderness. Even though they were a multitude, each one felt uniquely alone in the experience. You may be suffering a prolonged and fearful illness in your personal wilderness. Those you love surround and comfort you. Still, in the midst of the night … in the hours of painful treatment … in the swirling rush of your thoughts and emotions, you will, at times, feel alone. To find strength and peace in the wilderness, it is important to be surrounded with love, but, most important of all, you must be in deep fellowship with Me. In Me, you are never alone, and you are always dearly loved.

While illness can be a wilderness, there are many others. Losses, in many forms, can transform the richness of life into a barren wilderness overnight. These losses may include a financial downturn, taking your trusted financial supply out of your hands and out of your bank account. A dear friend or loved one, who has blessed your life with joy and affection, can suddenly become estranged and gone from your embrace or from your heart. A transfer of residence may take your precious ones far from your company. Death may disconnect you from a dear one in this life all together. Even the death of a dream is sufficient means to carry you to the boundary of the wilderness. The agony of the heart, and the confusion of the mind, can quickly transport you to the place that your soul would want to avoid.

Two questions fill your heart when you realize that you are standing in a barren place, where fear speaks incessantly and where accusation abounds. Two questions are swift to form in your mind: How did I get here? How can I find my way out? For some of My little ones, anger is the first emotion. In this state of heart the question becomes: What did I do to deserve this? Consider these questions with Me.

The demand to know **why** is nearly the same as the demand challenging the validity of one deserving such an uncomfortable and costly place. The question, of whether or not the discomfort is deserved, speaks a slightly different tone. It speaks of self-justification, while the other is just a cry for understanding. What is My reply to either question? I can answer with one word … LOVE. Because I love you, I will challenge you to greater growth and intimacy with Me. The wilderness experience will bring these two things to you if you give yourself fully to My purposes as you journey there. At the same time, when you rebel against My way, living out the inclinations of your fallen soul or out of the undelivered bondage contained there, it is always My love that is the foundation of My purposes for your time in the wilderness. Discipline and consequences are the manifestations of My love when a sheep is willful and disobedient … when the sheep is filled with pride and self-direction. If I did not love you, I would continue to allow you the benefits of your own sin, supplied from My enemy, to bless your rebellion. The harshness of the wilderness is a way to awaken you from the deception that has seized your soul. Even if the soul is not yet given into deep sin, but is following the path that will lead to it, I will redirect the steps to take the sheep into the wilderness. The wilderness is a message that says, 'Stop … awaken to take another course before perpetual pain and loss become your destination.'

Apart from the reason of sin, a journey into the wilderness can be a gift of training toward a promotion for My own. In the coming days there will be new threats to discern. There will be battles requiring new weapons and fresh strategies. An extraordinary level of obedience will be needed to provide the exceptional strength required to defeat the enemy. Training will bring into practice all that is required for success in the midst of war. If I did not love those whom I shepherd, I would let them learn as the challenges arise. Would this not lead to greater pain and heavier losses … to a prolonged battle with more casualties? It is certainly so. In the wilderness, the familiar is replaced with the demand to develop skills in the unfamiliar. Absolute obedience becomes the highest priority in war.

Consider the practice of worship and praise. The power of these things in battle is extraordinary when focused and operating as a weapon. Can these songs and activities become rote and familiar as the mind and the heart wander to focus elsewhere? Yes, this happens frequently in My flock. Rigid, set periods of time, and established songs and dances, can put boundaries around the level of worship. Control can dictate what is acceptable to Me and what level of practiced competency is necessary to please Me. The freedom of the human soul to worship without inhibition is curtailed. Soulish rules are enforced rather than holy order. Choral masters assume that their levels of human competency and performance are what I require. In many portions of the flock, there are people leading worship with a heart for it but not with the anointing from Me to do so. As a result, there is little power for warfare in this current activity called worship. There is little impact in My kingdom, as much of this worship activity does not even reach My place of habitation. In a time of war, the current application of this weapon will fail to serve unless it is transformed. I allow the worship times to be dry and unsatisfying. I allow for discord to abound in those enforcing human control over worship. I allow a barrenness of unity and a famine of true unbounded joy to accompany the current practice of worship. I bring forth this wilderness experience in order to guide the worshippers and their leaders to a new practice and to a new form of this weapon. The version that I offer is a surrendered, *new song* of spontaneity and a tone generated out of the Spirit. The songs and the dances that please Me are devoid of performance and consist only of adoration of Me. Those, who recognize that they are in the wilderness in this area of warfare, have the opportunity to avail themselves to the new as they lay aside the familiar. My flock has not yet seen the full power of this weapon to decimate the enemy and to secure victory for Me. To empower My worshippers, I offer the wilderness and the training found there. Those who refuse to enter into the teachings of the wilderness, to be broken by it, will not be able to enter into My presence to be empowered by it. I need for you to have My form of empowered worship in the time of war.

Willfulness … willfulness in My sheep creates a most certain road into the wilderness. Following the trail of deception laid by the enemy is another sure way into the barren wastelands. Know this: You will experience the wilderness differently if My hand has led you there. If your own rebellious, jealous, prideful, or deceitful heart has been forging your course, your self-directed journey into the wilderness will be far more painful than if you had allowed Me to take you there. I will still oversee your time in the barren places, but I will allow you to feel the cost of being there more keenly. Is that a cruelty? No. The surest way to break pride and rebellion is to allow My little ones to experience and to feel the consequences of such things. Rebellion is actually walking away from Me. Away from Me there is coldness, loneliness, empty rewards, and hollow relationships. Apart from Me, you will find a fragile and temporary prosperity that has been propped up by My enemy. You may be seeking a position of authority and rebelled against Mine. There will be little good or enduring fruit from your contrived leadership status. You may achieve a certain level of financial capability, but what you receive will neither satisfy you nor be retained by you. Anxiety will increase where you had hoped peace would be found. Whatever you build will shake and fall over time. You will eat and not ever be fully satisfied. Much of this pain will be the consequence of your rebellion. Some of it will be orchestrated by My hand, as My protection over you is temporarily lifted. You must learn that unholiness of heart, mind, or action will have a price in spiritual prosperity. You must come to experience the truth that physical or material prosperity, acquired through deceit or sin, will be empty when compared to the prosperity of the Spirit in Me.

Little ones, when you find yourself in the wilderness, come quickly to Me to discern why you are there. Do not assume that someone else has done this wicked thing to you. Do not even assume that you are being punished. Come and find out, in truth, regarding why you are in this condition. If you are open to hear truth, I will tell you these things clearly. Trust Me to release that revelation in the proper moment when My love sees fit to reveal it. If I delay in giving you the reason, which you are so earnestly seeking, trust Me. Truly, I will provide you with that information, even if it is not until right before your exit from that wilderness.

Listen, little ones. Learn what will help you acquire the bless-ings of the wilderness and, thereby, help you find your exit. First of all, do not run. Walk! Running in uncharted territory can increase your injury and hazard. Walking can allow you to observe the messages, which I have planted for you on the way. When the snakes and scorpions gather around your feet, focus on Me rather than upon them. If you do not give your heart to the threat and fear they speak, they will not poison you. Continue to walk until I tell you to lie down to rest. To lie down where I have not told you to rest your head will put you in great danger. Seek the shelter that I alone give you. Do not rush into an available cave to get out of the storm. A devour-ing threat can be lying in wait for you within that cave. Do not drink from water sources other than from Mine. Do not allow your thirst to drive your soul to drink from unholy wells and streams. Abide in your thirst until I give you My living water. When the thorn branches gather and crowd around your head, get low. Humility will guard your mind from the pride-ful lies that may have led you to this place.

Be careful to carry nothing upon your back. Too often, My little ones try to carry another person along on this journey to be a comfort and to be company. Be willing to be alone with Me during this time. Entrust all other people into My care. Stay in the present so that you can hear, from Me, the things from your past which have led you to this wilderness. Walk forward without looking backwards. If there is something behind you, which is important for you to know, I will deliver that information to you. Carry nothing in your hands. Carry no weapons of self-protection, for I am your Protector. Carry no earthly books for comforting reference, but keep My word ever in your heart and ever on your mind. Listen for the words of My Spirit teaching you as you journey. Eat the food that I bring to you, and receive it from the source, which I have chosen to bring it to you. Even a bird can be My servant to feed you. If the food is not to your liking, eat it anyway for it will strengthen and heal you. As parts of yourself break in your stumbling along the way, allow them to be broken, and allow for Me to heal them. If portions of your understanding shatter … if parts of your heart break … even if your feet give out underneath you, all is well. If I allow these things to happen, they must happen. You are to emerge from the wilderness as a new and restored lamb. Allow this Shepherd to lead you through the wilderness, providing for you in every way.

Know this: As you are cut and injured along the way, I am willing to suffer the same things as I walk with you. If you choose to suffer apart from Me, you will suffer alone until you learn that, without Me to share it, the suffering is too great to bear. Know that there is nothing that you will suffer in the wilderness which I have not also suffered on your behalf. I was broken and rejected. I was torn and mocked. I was accused when without fault. I have known every temptation and carried the greatest pain. I have experienced a time of separation that you could never bear. Know that My eyes are always upon you. Every step you make is keenly observed. Every moment is equipped with a gift toward your wholeness. Pick up each gift and draw it into your heart's embrace, even if it appears to be a thorn of truth to hurt you. Trust My way.

The wilderness is not to be your final destination. It is meant to be a way to get you to that ultimate victory. If you have taken yourself into the dry places, be quick to repent, so that I can bring you the brokenness and the healing necessary to restore you. If I have brought you in to take you upwards in your authority, simply yield to the course which I have laid for you through the wilderness.

So … is the wilderness a penalty or is it a promotion? You have the power to decide the outcome by the posture of the soul you assume in the midst of the wilderness. I offer it to you as a blessing. It can drive from you the sin and oppression that have kept you weak. It can create muscle strength of the spirit. It can provide new eyes and sharpened ears for finding provision and blessing in hidden places. It can bring you and Me into a deeper intimacy than you ever thought possible. You decide what it will be by the posture you assume. Will you enter in with the mind and heart of submitted, obedient humility? Will you be thrown into the briars by your own rebellious heart and then choose to find your own way out? I have provided a way for all of you through the wilderness. Will you accept it, or will you curse it and, in doing so, choose to dwell there? Either way, I am in the wilderness, staying nearby. I am your answer. I am the way through the wilderness … there is no other.

PASSING SHADOWS

Little ones, what happens when you take a perfect piece of fruit and hold it in your hand? It might be a peach or a pear, an apple or a banana. As you hold it and smell it, your appetite to eat it may grow. If it seems too perfect to eat, or if your stomach is too full, you may want to keep it for later. How long will it remain beautiful and delicious? Over time, the hidden imperfections will begin to become evident. Perhaps there is a bit of hidden mold around the stem. Maybe the fruit has the tiniest indentation, which will later give evidence of a bruise hidden underneath it. Any little microbe on the surface or under the skin will begin to thrive in the environment of sweet sugar that increases as the fruit ages. Tiny little insects will soon swarm around your piece of overripe fruit, announcing to you that you have kept it too long uneaten. Eventually, even the most perfect piece of fruit will wither or turn rotten over time. What if the fruit in your hand is seen as clearly blemished from your first glance? It will spoil so much more quickly.

What is the substance of things surrounding you in the world, little ones? Is it the substance out of which eternal, permanent things arise? Just like your piece of fruit, this world was not intended to remain forever. It has blemishes that are obvious and hidden rot outside of your view. The world, as it now stands, must pass away. And with its passing, all that is sinful and soiled… all that is corrupt and evil will pass away. Is there anything so dear among these things of impermanence which you would choose to hold rather than release? Would you ever want these things in their fallen state to become eternal? Out of My love and mercy … out of My holiness, I would never allow it.

Familiar … that is what these things are to you. These things of earthly substance are familiar, and, in that familiarity, you often find a comfort to your soul. There might even be the sense of a sort of kinship between the things of the earth and yourself.

Over time, this human creation has compensated for the decay of corruption as it spread from civilization to civilization … from generation to generation. First, the excuses for the moral decay arose from the minds to be declared from the mouths of the people. This was followed by an acceptance and later even by a perverse honor for successful wickedness. If the world would be allowed to continue on this course unchecked, would this not lead to the blatant worship of evil? Is it not already being seen? I cannot allow this, for such a direction is the way of eternal separation from Me.

The delusion has become so firmly planted in some human minds, believing that the substance of the earth is both holy and eternal, that the earth is revered as deity and is worshipped. Some of My created children already make daily sacrifices to the planet. Their worship of that which has been created blinds them to real deity. The priority of their lives has become the maintenance of the planet earth, even to the degree that they battle other humans who believe in the sanctity of the human lives dwelling upon the earth. 'Above all else,' they say, 'the planet earth must continue.' Therefore, all those who threaten its continuance … even those who rightly use My word to say, 'all this will pass away' … are scorned and attacked. Whom should the sons of men be attacking? Against whom should the daughters of men be lifting up their voices to decry? The world has become greatly skewed. The minds of men are darkened and bent. Their eyes are blind. The hearts of men are twisted and cold. The understandings of men are formed into celebrated falsehoods, which are declared as deep truths. Should not all of these corrupted things pass away?

If I created all things, could I not recreate them and restore to them their original purity? Could I not restore to the world its former beauty? I can and I shall, but only when the things you see before you now pass away. Do not grieve their passing. Only grieve for those of the human creation who will refuse to be recreated by My truth and love. Those who refuse will abide in the evil and in the corruption which they have chosen over both wholeness and holiness.

Hold the things of this world loosely, little ones, for, truly, before your eyes, the things of this world are passing away. Rejoice! The substance that shall come forth to replace all which is passing away will be of the eternal perfection which I have promised in My word. Even the parts of yourself that are flawed and dark shall be replaced by perfection. You shall, in the process, not become god as the false ones profess, but, in My light, you shall both know and reflect Me.

What of your pain, blindness, delusion, and misery would you wish to be eternal? Of course, you would choose none of these if asked. Why then do you behave to the contrary? Why then, little ones, do you fight so hard against surrendering your imperfections to the process of being broken and released in order to be made whole? Are you so unwilling to let these damaged and corrupted things pass away? Do you see these darkened areas of your life as the substance of who you are? Are you deceived into thinking that, in having what you evaluate as the gold of your soul exposed to be seen as the brass it really is, you would lose and even negate who you are?

Foolish children, you live now as a shadow. There will be no shadows in My eternal Kingdom. Being exposed to the light that comes from only one direction will always cast a shadow. Rather choose to be exposed totally to the light, which surrounds completely and penetrates absolutely, so that no shadow is possible. Do not be afraid of such light. This is the light of My brightness … the true presence which shall expose all of your darkness. Come, despise the darkness and long for it to pass away. Does the unknown frighten you? Do you wonder … 'who shall I be when the shadows, in which I can now hide, are all gone?'

Who seeks to convince you that your fear is based upon truth? Which voice do you hear telling you to avoid this process by which your old nature passes away? What voice speaks to you in admiration and in comfort concerning your private darkness? Listen carefully, and you shall hear a sickeningly sweet hiss, mingled with your own voice of self-righteousness, calling you to self-protection and to self-preservation. Which would you prefer to be eternal: your fallen self, or your self fully restored to holiness? Your decision will determine where you will experience eternity. Will it be within My holy city, or will it be beyond its walls with the outcasts? Be quick to determine your choice, for, truly I say, both the Refiner's fire and the eternal fire are at hand. Choose where you will enter in and where you will abide. For these things of the world are passing away and with them will be all things of shadow and darkness. The dawn of eternity will come as all these things of imperma- nence and unholiness pass away. The fruit of your life which remains will endure for eternity. Choose!

DESPERATION

Little ones, what does it mean to be desperate? Do you remember a time in your life when your soul felt infused with desperation? Think back. What caused the feeling of desperation to seize your heart and mind? What situation of fear presented itself to your life and then proceeded to hold your mind and heart in its grasp? Did the feeling of desperation come upon you suddenly, or did it creep in slowly until it was a full manifestation in your soul? Is desperation merely anxiety? Is it only an expression of worry? In your time of desperation, did you find also an element of hopelessness and a sense of being overwhelmed causing you to become frantic?

Desperation, as it turns you to Me, can be a doorway to comfort and liberation. However, if you cling to desperation in search of your own doorway to relief from the oppression of your soul, you will play directly into the hands of a debilitating enemy. If you are too slow in recognizing a desperate situation, trying to make a stand against challenging circumstances in your own flesh, you can quickly be swallowed up and carried away in both soul and body.

Little ones, the world is moving toward a time of desperate days. The great clash of kingdoms, which has occurred since the beginning of sin, is moving toward a great apex. Human flesh will fail to find solutions to the overwhelming challenges. Worldly supply will fail to provide the needs of either body or soul. Where, then, will the hearts of My children turn in their time of desperation? It is good to consider these things now, before the depth of these realities comes to consume your world.

It is written that My grace is sufficient for you. Do you believe those words and do you live out of that truth now? In a time of desperation, you must draw from an unquestionable sufficiency. If you rely upon any element of human ability to be even a portion of your sufficiency, you will find your resources lacking as the desperation of the coming days comes to enter into your house.

So many of My children rely upon locks, bolts, and security systems to keep their lives and possessions safe. They sleep at night in peace, in the belief that these measures will keep them and their surrounding world safe. They leave their home in the confidence that everything will be as it was when they departed and locked their doors. What if a frayed wire releases a spark in the midst of their walls while they are absent or as they sleep? What if an earthquake comes to shake the foundations of their house to the point of crumbling the doorposts containing their locks … to the point where the electronic devices are crushed? What if a flood invades or if a whirlwind descends to visit destruction upon the house? Will the locks and the alarms hold back the devastation such events bring with them? Do you see, little ones, the insufficiency of your

own security measures in the day of great peril? Do you realize the futility of self-protection in the days of overwhelming
trouble? Know this: the human devices that have worked for
you in the days of normal threat and challenge will prove to
be inadequate in the days of desperation upon the earth.

The human mind can only devise solutions to a certain extent. It can only process facts to a limited degree of understanding. Human legs can only outrun a pursuing threat for a
limited time and only at a limited speed. The human heart can
only carry the weight of a limited amount of emotional challenge. In the human being, there are boundaries established
beyond which a person cannot achieve. I established those
boundaries, designing human abilities to end at the very place
where My power is available for My children to excel. It is at
this juncture where your salvation comes or where your desperation consumes you.

At the very place where human abilities come to an end,
the powers of the supernatural arise. Those powers, which
exist in the spiritual plane, are positioned to meet human in-
adequacy, enabling the human being to proceed beyond individual human abilities. It is at this juncture where you have
the opportunity to choose My help, to choose the help of the
satanic kingdom, or to refuse all help. Choices must be made
in desperate times. What will you choose?

If finding consolation is your priority in the face of great challenges to your comfort, you will find support available to you
from both My kingdom and from the powers of evil. Those
who consider their choice simply on the basis of getting results, will see that evil powers are able to provide results, but
they will fail to see the high cost of choosing to receive this
support. Consider the source that is providing the results you
are hoping to find. Evil can bring temporary comfort while

hiding from your view the price in torment and great loss attached to the fine print in the agreement. Desperation has a tendency to encourage rash and unwise decisions to alleviate discomfort and fear in the most immediate way. The human soul gravitates toward expediency in distress. Beware of being led by your soul in the days of great challenge.

Consider the results being demanded by your soul in the days of distress. If the immediate need is safety, you may choose to run to a false tower to escape a threat. If the tower in which you seek safety is not Mine, how secure will you be … how long will you be safe? Perhaps, what is shown to you by darkness is only an illusionary tower, but is in reality a cage. A time will come when you will have to choose between an illusion of safety and a life of integrity and truth. In the distress of your soul, be careful not to seek safety for your life while laying aside the truth of who you are called to be in the world. The uplifting hand that I offer is given quickly to those who live in truth and in integrity. What result would you prefer … safety in the temporal or victory in the eternal? There is always safety in My eternal Kingdom. In a crisis, if My Kingdom is your priority and if truth and integrity are the desired end results, choosing My help will be easy.

In preparing for desperate days I have told you to have your priorities established in an immovable place. I have told you to be ready to make choices that will allow Me to provide all that you need. I have cautioned you against being led by your own flesh and directed by your own soul. I have warned you against waiting too long to recognize your need. I have assured you that I will meet you at the boundary of your insufficiency. What more should I say to you about these coming days of desperation?

Do not fear being in a place of desperation, little ones. In the midst of this distress of soul and body, be desperate for Me. Know that, in the final days of distress upon the world, My grace will abound to you as never before. You will hear the clash of nations and you will see the threats of war made manifest upon the earth. Darkness will arise in an attempt to suffocate all that is truthful, good, and holy. Even now, it is arising in unprecedented ways. You will hear of encroaching plagues and you will feel the ground under your feet rise and fall. In these moments, where the soul wants to leap into a place of security, leap into My arms. When the air of the world becomes acrid and poisonous, allow Me to fill you with My breath. Be desperate for it and you will receive it. When your storehouse is empty of food, dine upon Me. It is written that I will lead My flock to pastures of abundant, good food. Trust in that. You will find yourself alone at times, with no ally at hand and with no one to share the agony of your heart. I am here for you. My presence will surround you as in no other time in the history of the world. Be desperate for Me in the midst of your desperation. When your mind cannot hold the horrors that your eyes behold and your ears have heard, take My mind within you to process these things. Do not reply upon your own soul's interpretation of reality. At times, your own heart will be inclined to abandon all hope as the world spins out of control in manifested evil. Let your heart be fixed on My truth, that evil will not prevail against My own, for they are hidden away in a secret place of the spirit.

These days of peril and desperation upon the earth must come as they have been foretold, but they will pass quickly. Like a great body vomiting up an ingested poison, the world will retch and recoil. It will heave and sway and then fall. When evil will have done its best to seize My possession, My Kingdom will arise in great power and crush the enemy. Those who have apprehended My grace will arise in great victory.

Evil desperation will have departed, being replaced by a desperate desire in the world for holiness and truth.

Can you see these things in your spirit now, little lambs? Do you feel the quickening of truth in your soul? Be watchful, but be expectant of wonders yet to come. Take note of the anxiety arising in your heart, as the news of world events is given to your soul to consider. Place encroaching doubt and dread under your feet of faith. When those around you begin to scurry in frantic self-protection, lean back against My chest and listen to the beat of My heart in perfect rhythm. Lie down to sleep in the center of My great palm and inhale a great breath of My Spirit. I have chosen you to walk through these days upon the earth, therefore, I have equipped you to walk them out in victory. You will be My voice of truth in the midst of deception and swirling lies. You will be a demonstration of order and wholeness in a world of chaotic fractionation. When the world is desperate for human power and for human answers to bring relief, you will abide in My all-sufficient grace, desperate only for Me to shepherd you through the darkness into the victorious light. In these truths, be at peace, little ones. Be at peace.

MECHANICAL HEARTS

Little ones, how is your heart beating in this moment? Is the rate fast? Is it beating at a restful pace? Since the beginning of human life upon the earth, My children have been fascinated by the mystery of the human heart. Its life sustaining beat can be felt and heard doing its faithful work of pumping life throughout a physical body, moment by moment. I have told you that your heart beat is the ticking clock of your life. Only I know when each clock will ultimately cease its rhythmic endeavor.

The mechanics of the heart have always been the focus of great fascination for My little ones. Until technology was able to discern its operation, this precious organ remained a mystery ... the subject of many theories. The one consistent proven reality was that if the heart stopped, life left the body to be replaced by death. Gradually, as time passed, some of the mysteries of the physical heart were unlocked. In mercy, I sent forth wisdom and understanding, revelation and skill, placing keys into the hands of physicians, enabling the repair of a sick or damaged heart. In time, it was revealed that the heart could be temporally stopped, its work briefly assigned to a machine, so that the natural pump of life could be surgically restored. I have allowed many damaged physical hearts to be repaired in this way, extending both the days of life and their quality. Still, there were so many more mysteries yet to be uncovered. In time, the death of one person became the doorway of hope for another. I placed in the minds and into hands of physicians the ability to remove a strong heart from one, whose life could be extended no longer, and placed into the chest of another, so that the renewal of life and hope could be given. Before long, transplanting the heart of someone passing from life to one who would die without the gift, became a daily operation. Quickly, this wonder was shown to have a limitation. To those in need, the human heart for transplant quickly became a vital commodity … a necessary pump in short supply. An alternative to My natural creation was again sought. It entered into the minds of researchers to acquire the heart of an animal to beat in the chest of a human being. Intellectual practicality and pride sought to move this technology beyond the limits I set in My word, dooming it to eventual failure. New possibilities and questions again began forming within the human soul. 'Perhaps we can extend life indefinitely if we create a mechanical organ to replace the one of mere muscle.' The exploration of electrical impulses, structure, and mechanics brought forth an artificial, mechanical heart. Even now, blood is being circulated through the bodies of the recipients of these man-made hearts. Have I been replaced by witty invention? No … even though there are humans who believe that to be true. I have allowed this technology so that My children would have a parable speaking of some far greater needs being unmet in the deeper human heart.

Follow Me now, as I speak to you of the mechanical human heart in spiritual terms. Consider the heart of the soul rather than the physical muscle that beats within your chest.

The invisible heart of soul and spirit, placed within each of you, is also intended to beat in a rhythm established by Me. However, I have set this heart of soul free to be under the authority of human choice and free will. It can beat in My rhythm or in a rhythm of its own choice and design. My Word is a guide book ... a users' manual, designed to instruct each person in the course and care of a healthy soul. Unlike the physical heart, the soul heart is designed to grow larger: increasing its boundaries as love nourishes it and as times passes. The more love that pumps through the heart, the more enduring and the more powerful this heart becomes. As the various life experiences flow through the soul, sometimes the heart can become damaged or diseased. As the Creator, I am also the Great Heart Physician. While I often heal directly from My hand, I have also trained faithful practitioners to be My touch, My voice, and My healing balm when heart repair is needed. Beware, little ones ... do not entrust your heart to heart practitioners who are not taught and led by My Spirit, or your mending may be temporary. It may even be detrimental to you. Improper diagnosis, or treatments arising from human understanding, may build up that which needs to be removed, or remove that which must be allowed to stay for you to grow to maturity. Allow Me to guide you in this matter.

Even as a physical heart is greatly affected by what you eat in your diet, so, also, is the soul heart. Be careful of the diet you present to your heart. Self-indulgence, pride, discontent, carnality, and rebellion are just a few of the deadly items I frequently see on your plates. Whatever you watch, whatever captures your ears' attention, whatever you touch, and whatever you take into your soul as truth will affect the growth, strength, and health of your heart. I have told you to dine upon things that are lovely, worthy, truthful, righteous, and pure. The virus of deception comes in many tasty forms, attractive to the human soul. Know the ingredients and the origin of the food you offer up for your soul's ingestion.

Often when the soul's heart has been damaged by diet or by life experience, the human urgently wants to be rid of the painful consequence or effects of these things. Rather than embracing the healing processes I have established, the inclination is often to close off that portion of the heart, which is suffering. Soon, that portion becomes useless as the defensive wall rising around it confines it, removing it from the healing flow of love and truth. If the soul makes the choice to withhold forgiveness to someone, life in that portion of the heart shrivels and dies. If the soul makes the choice to embrace and to live out of a lie, rather than out of the truth, a portion of that heart will harden against both love and truth. Remember this: any love supported by deception and deceit is a false love. The task I have given to the heart, to bring forth love as its choice, becomes re-assigned to the authority of the mind, where reality can be cast by woundedness into a mold which agrees with the wounded, deceived heart.

Where one portion of the soul's heart has been shut down or recreated by deceptions of the mind, the created heart is slowly replaced by an artificial heart. Bit by bit … portion by portion, the divinely created heart of the soul becomes something that is dependent upon an externally made reality and structure. It relies on an artificial power source other than Me. While the illusion prospers that this mechanical heart is better, more practical, and more durable, it is in fact much weaker than the one I give you. An artificial heart cannot discern the truths that arise from My Spirit. It cannot embrace My truth, which brings forth the element of hope. Therefore, an artificial heart is deficient of hope. Life itself becomes more burdensome; as My child seeks to carry around the burden and the bulk of things needed to sustain an alternative, artificial heart ... one that operates contrary to My design, lacking My substance.

What burdens will the recipient of a mechanical heart carry? Self-protection replaces My protection in the life of this little one. Fear adds oppressing dimensions to the heavy load of insecurity and worry. The lack of true love flowing through a mechanical heart brings a deficiency of joy and peace. A lack of love flowing through and nourishing that heart will cause the vision of the soul's eyes to be dimmed and out of focus. When true love enters in, it often cannot be absorbed to feed the hungry soul. In the place of love, manipulation, greed, control, and jealousy feed the operations of the mechanical heart. Legalism enters in to keep the moving parts of this system in motion. All the while, the mind has been telling the emotions and assuring the dysfunctional responses that indeed all is well.

Rather than having a totally artificial heart, perhaps there is only a small portion of the heart that has been replaced with the substitute. If that is the condition ... if most of the heart is operational according to My creation, but only one area of the heart is false ... what then is the risk? Authenticity ... that is what is at risk. Whatever needed to be healed or excised to bring full health has been hidden by artificial structures, giving the illusion of intact health and life. To the untrained eye, this falsehood may be undetected until a challenge is made which addresses that specific portion of the heart function. Meanwhile, underneath the presented reality, there is a secret ... something false, weak, and artificial, even if it is only known to Me and to that little one. The love is not authentic and the function is a false representation of wholeness. Consider it in this way: A hand may be able to operate fairly well without one finger. The efforts of the other fingers can often compensate for the loss, that is, unless the missing finger is a thumb. The loss of that specific finger cannot be covered by the others. An artificial thumb can be applied, but the integrity of the naturally created hand is nevertheless impaired. When I bring healing to address the damage within My children, I do not bring prosthetics or supports to prop up what is false or hidden. I bring healing that restores integrity of soul and authenticity to My little ones.

Do you have a fresh understanding of these things now? To bring more clarity, perhaps you need to consider the symptoms which arise as an outworking from this artificiality of heart. The heart of soul has been designed to be powered by love. Obedience, sacrifice, gentleness, strength, passion, commitment, endurance, actions, and words are to arise out of the flow of love through the soul heart of My children. When portions of that heart are artificial, evidence of that fact will eventually emerge. Is the service being rendered to someone the result of love, or is there something else empowering the action? If a portion of that heart has been wounded by rejection, service can come forth out of an artificial structure set up by the mind to be the proof of importance and accepted inclusion. Generosity can be offered to cover up a wound left by this same element of rejection. The generous service may be seen as coming forth empowered by love, when in reality it may be offered to meet a personal need, which was created by a spirit of insignificance or a fear of abandonment. If an outpouring of affirmation and gratitude does not come forth to the donor from the recipient of this blessing of generous service, offense and anger often arise in that soul. The response will often reveal the artificial nature of the heart's gesture. The hidden intentions may come forth when the need, hidden behind the artificial, is left frustrated or unsatisfied.

For a moment, consider with Me the issue of legalism. The law in My Word was given to be a guide leading you to fulfillment, to wisdom, to safety, and to blessing. Your pursuit of any holy observance of these requirements is to be a gift of your love given to Me, demonstrated by your joyful obedience. Observance of My commands were never meant to be a form of self-promotion or self-recommendation in the eyes of others. I look at your heart as you engage in your practices and observances. If the motivation is not honor, love, adoration, and holy awe toward Me supporting your activities, these things may not be honoring Me at all. If you participate in the dictates arising from the suppositions and rulings formed out of the minds of men, rather than from what is actually written in My word, you may be participating in hollow rituals. If what you do both honors Me and draws you to love and know Me more, I am pleased. Your actions and words are to present a testimony of My love and reality to others. However, if what you do in your religious observance has become comfortable rote, set pattern, without the investment of heart … without your relationship with Me and with others being deepened in truth and love … you may have another priority, other than Mine, in place. Before going beyond what I have clearly demanded for your life practices, be discerning of your motives and heart. I am not blessed by hollow traditions and rituals. If you find your identity and affirmation in these things, rather than in Me, you are operating out of a mechanical, artificial heart. Eventually these things will break down. They must, because they are not created of eternal substance, nor offered up in humble devotion.

Rid yourself of this artificiality that distances you from Me and from others. Stop lifting up your standard for acceptance and holiness in lieu of Mine. My Word does not need to be edited or augmented. My Spirit will lead you in its truth. Putting on man-made yokes of required practice, intending to please Me, often only distances you from Me and from those in great need to know Me, as they observe you. It is good enough that true obedience to My Word may make you look foolish in the eyes of the world. Do not allow your own foolish notions to speak poorly of Me. Search your heart and My Word ... allow Me to search you with My Spirit. I will show you what is the foolish substance of well intending minds and what is true honor given to Me. Artificial hearts do not add to My Kingdom, nor do they bring life-giving truth to those in need.

Precious little ones, My enemy seeks continually to mislead you, causing you to embrace that which is false. He seeks to tie you up in laws and systems and in theories about life with Me, in order to make you irrelevant to the needy world. He wants you to live interiorly self-concerned, while casting an impression to others that you have a life rich with truth and faith. Your façade can be easily seen. My enemy wants you to be so concerned with the things which I do not require, that you will neglect My clear mandates. He wants you so full of pride and driven by ulterior motives, that your hearts will become mechanical and artificial ... always in a deficit of love. Full well he knows that only the actions you make out of a heart of genuine love will be recorded in My eternal book of righteous and lauded deeds.

Put your hand upon your chest. Do you feel the rhythm of the interior clock within you? Do you feel the physical power propelling life throughout your body? For what reason does that heart beat? Is there anything in your heart or soul that is false? Have artificial parts been installed in order that you might feel more secure, significant, or protected? Wherever the artificial has been given a place of authority, no authentic truth can abide. Beloved, you were not made by rote. You were individually crafted and tuned to My purposes. You were created by the hands of authentic love. You are the genuine article. That true portion is still alive under all that is artificial. Give Me your heart. Allow Me to reveal to you the things that are mechanical, artificial, and false. You may feel some pain as I break off the rigid walls, grids, and supports … removing the artificial portions of your heart … but I will do this in loving mercy. Never be afraid of the real and authentic truth. My heart's cry is that you would come to know Me, embracing Me in spirit and in truth. Come work in agreement with Me. Soon I will reveal to you a deeper revelation of eternal things, shown only to those pure in heart, following My greatest command. Without a trace of ulterior motive, simply LOVE. Freely, with genuine transparent, self-abandonment, truly love. What? You cannot do that? Oh, little ones … I know that full well. Give me your heart, so that I can make it Mine. There … with your genuine choice and with My perfect ability it is accomplished.

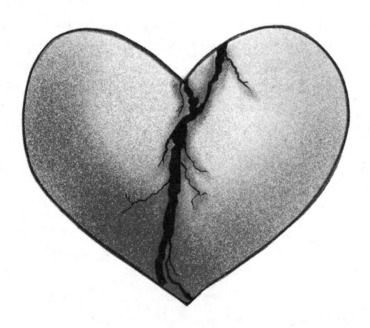

A BROKEN AND CONTRITE HEART

Little ones, the matters of your heart have been a great priority for Me. Out of your heart your mouth speaks, and, out of that heart, actions arise: producing life or death. As I AM all Life, I want you to reflect that life within you. Perceptions and conclusions are so powerful in formulating your realities. You rely upon them to lead you to truth, when often they take you down an opposite road, away from the truth you seek.

Is it not true that you are well aware of the times when others have broken your heart ... when they have disappointed you or hurt you? When you are the one who has received a blow, it is easy to perceive it. When you deliver a blow to another person, often the truth of it escapes your awareness. If you have been angry with that person, the delivery of a counter punch can seem justified, even bringing joyful satisfaction in the awareness that you have been empowered to impact another with the message of your displeasure. Such counter-punches grieve Me greatly, for this is not the way of My Kingdom.

I have told you that all must come into My Kingdom as a little child and grow into maturity and stature over time. However, the precious child within you is always to remain as an operative part of your being. I love your exuberant joy and your playful curiosity, little ones. I love your trust and your sense of obedient adventure reflecting your childlike heart. My cry is for you to remain childlike, but to abandon all child-ishness. But even as a child in immaturity, often your actions and words impact others in a hurtful or uncomfortable way, without your knowledge of that fact. Often you consider matters of SELF first, over and above the consideration of others. That has been common in the state of My human children ever since they embarked upon the road to independence apart from My truth at the enticement of the great deceiver. I now want you to consider the way of return that will take you to a state of heart where the childlike abounds, but where the childish nature is not found.

It is written: A broken and contrite heart I will not despise. What does that mean to you and to your life, little ones? To be broken translates out as something that is shattered and no longer useful in its current state. It speaks of needed repair or replacement. You work hard to maintain the function of mechanical things, lest brokenness would render them use-less. Brokenness is something that, your mind tells you, must be avoided. Yet, in My Kingdom, brokenness of heart is a ne-cessity. You see, the pride of the carnal heart creates a barrier against the things of My Kingdom. The carnal constructions of the human ego work contrary to the way of My heart. All that which is prideful, self-made, hard, and selfish must be broken before the character of My heart, and before the re-flection of My Kingdom, can be manifested through you. This brokenness is not optional.

A contrite heart is one that is penitent: a heart which is

self-aware of the sin that arises from it, forming actions and words that hurt My heart and others. A contrite heart bows before Me and seeks forgiveness for the rebellion, pride, and sin which arise from the flesh so easily. A contrite heart is a heart that humbly seeks truth about the self, so that it might draw more closely to Me, to be conformed into the way of My heart. Therefore, a broken heart … one which has had its self-willed hardness shattered … is the way to obtain a contrite heart. An unbroken heart stands up proud and self-justifying. Contrition is not possible in such a heart. A broken and contrite heart is a precious sacrifice, which you can offer up to Me. Such a sacrifice tells Me that I am more important as your priority, than you are to yourself. When I am the highest priority … when I surpass the priority of your own soul … your whole life becomes transformed into Kingdom glory.

So, little ones, how can you test whether your heart is contrite and broken? The easiest test it to note how you respond to an offense. What is the priority that pops to the surface, to present itself as your first manifestation, in reply to the perceived offense? Does anger rise in your heart, whether or not it pours out from your lips? Allow Me to explore that more deeply. How do you see that person and the words that have offended you? Do you see the needs being expressed in that other person before you focus upon your own needs? Do you see the pain in the one who has offended you, or is your own pain the top priority? Do you automatically see the intentions of the heart as evil toward you, or do you extend mercy and grace to accommodate an accidental offense or error on the part of the offender? Do you see the possibility that your inclination to pick up offense might be the result of an unrelated historical wound still unhealed within you? Is there something operating within you that is inclined to see and hear the negative, even when it is not being expressed? Is your first response forgiveness if the intention to hurt you is truthfully made evident? Your angry response can be as great a sin in My eyes, as the hurtful actions or words of offense presented to you by another.

So often the issue of offense involves the matter of ascendancy. Who is superior? Who has more right, more power, more truth, or more control? Who has more authority? Too often these matters of offense are manifestations out of a kind of sibling rivalry, arising as My insecure children battle each other to prove themselves to be higher, more honored, or more beloved than the other. Such behavior and such priorities grieve My heart. Power is so often the issue. The demand to have status and rights acknowledged will often consume a darkened heart and mind to interpret what is innocent as if it is a threat.

But, 'What if there is real threat?', you ask. My question back to you, little one, is this: What actually comprises a <u>real</u> threat to your life and to your position in truth? Much of what you perceive as a threat is nothing more than flesh seeking ascendancy and affirmation. Things that threaten your body or your health ... even these things are My concern to care for you. Seek My help and My defense in these physical threats. Dismiss the challenges, which threaten your ego, rights, and position, as merely refining moments. I am the defense of the truth that abides within you. I will vindicate you, if you abide in Me. If someone challenges your identity, do not fear, if your identity is established in Me. Your true identity will prove itself as I show Myself to be foundational within your being. Stop responding to offense as if you must respond in order to vindicate yourself, or to prove yourself. The true substance of your being will give evidence in your words and actions over time. As I comprise more of your substance, the evidence of that reality will visibly appear to convince those who seek truth.

For those who shun truth, nothing you could ever say or do, apart from Me, would ever convince them. Remember, there is no threat to your survival which arises without My awareness. My hand remains upon you, as long as you do not choose to step out from under My sovereign Lordship over your life.

Know this truth: The proper response to a hurtful attack of words and actions is not anger if I am your Lord. The appropriate response is tears … but not tears for your own pain… tears for the oppression, delusion, or pain in the one attacking you. Forgiveness extended to those who do not understand what they are doing or saying is the reply of one, who abides in My heart. Tears of sadness and grief, concerning the stranglehold maintained by My enemy over the one attacking you, is the sign of a surrendered and compassionate, Kingdom heart. This precious heart allows Me to deal with the attack according to My purposes in the moment. Perhaps, I will arise to speak forth words of powerful, loving, truth through your lips to unseat the enemy in the life of that person attacking you. Perhaps I will choose to demonstrate the heart of a servant, as you swallow your pride and surrender your defense into My hands, remaining quiet. I alone know the specific counterpunch that needs to be made in the Spirit, in order to unseat the enemy in any situation. Is that your goal in a conflict … to unseat the enemy, or is the goal to vindicate yourself and to secure your own position and power? You get to choose the direction the conflict resolution will take.

A broken and contrite heart will weep for those who challenge or hurt it. It will not be a manipulative weeping: drawing attention to the self or seeking to bring condemnation upon the other. The weeping, which I seek from you, and the tears which flow from Me on your behalf, are tears of true compassion. This compassion seeks the best for the attacker. These tears see the pain within the attacker … the delusion, the abuse, the fear, and the lack of affirmation, which have set this attack into motion from a deep place in the soul. The heart cry is for both healing and forgiveness, as My child recognizes the deep needs within the one who brutalizes and shuns.

Do you see, now, how vital a broken and contrite heart is before Me? It is this kind of heart that mirrors My heart of servant love. It is this heart that can submit all suffering experienced to Me, so that I might hold, restore, and vindicate. It is one with a broken and contrite heart … the one, who has seen his or her own sin clearly … the one, who can have compassion for one sinning against him or her. This is the heart that pleases Me … the heart that presents the testimony of My heart.

The broken and contrite heart is precisely the heart needed for successful intercession and for petition. It is a heart that is self-aware and, also, aware of others, acknowledging both as those, who likewise are inclined to sin and hurt. The broken and contrite heart is one that I can work through powerfully to change the world. It is also the heart that draws most closely to Me.

Little ones, I want you to be free, whole, safe, and honored. At the same time, I am the only Way that these things can come into your life. Lay down the arrogant ego within you that stands up to challenge My Lordship … the ego, which guards your rights and your position before others … the ego that seeks to prove and to vindicate yourself. Give Me that broken heart, which has been torn by the words and actions of others, so that I might heal it as you forgive and bless. In this way, you will be more conformed into My image. In this way, you will arise in like manner as a Restorer of others. You see, it was my choice to become intimately familiar with life as a human being, so that I would show you the sure path to victory over your enemy. In My Kingdom the low path is actually the HIGH path of the overcomer.

Brokenness is the way to wholeness. Weakness can become the pathway to the greatest strength. Spiritual authority comes to those who release their human authority to acquire Mine. Tears of the broken become a powerful force to erode the prison walls established by the evil one.

So, little ones … do you now understand that, in My Kingdom, that which is broken and restored by My hand is the MOST functional and the MOST useful? Do not fear being broken according to My plan for your life. Do not judge My breaking process going on in the lives of others. Surrender to My wisdom. See yourself and others as I see, not according to your flesh. The resulting change in you will be profound. The Kingdom power and authority you will carry will glorify Me, not yourself. Your enemies will have a far more difficult time baiting you into a rage that would lead you to defeat. And you, dear one, will come to know true peace and wholeness. This is My heart cry for you. Give me all the pain and offense. Turn to Me in the dreadful challenges. Give into My keeping all those hurtful words and actions, which have wounded your heart. Give to me the pain, and the impressions of sorrow and injustice that you carry from the past, lest they color the truth of your present reality. As I heal you, a new strength will arise in you. The sacrifice that you give to Me will not be wasted but will bear much fruit. My hands are open to receive your heart. Are you willing to surrender all of it to My love?

THE BUTTERFLY'S BATTLE

Little ones, do you ever feel as if you are earthbound or stuck in a place where you never seem to be able to change? Do you feel as if you are crawling, while others around you are flying? Do you ever feel ugly, while viewing others as being so much more beautiful than you are? These are frequently imposed, false perceptions sent from the great deceiver. My enemy wants you to feel rejected, worthless, trapped, 'less than,' and hopeless. To achieve his goal, he speaks dark deceptions into your life situations and condemnations into your personhood. If you become locked up in self-pity, saturated with self-condemnation, or self-consumed by discontent, you will be unavailable to serve Me. Your eyes will become so focused upon the carnal that you become blind to the glorious work that I am doing in you and around you.

Surely, the lowly little caterpillar could sympathize with your desperation. That motley, dusty brown, little caterpillar looks very plain and unremarkable standing next to a brightly colored beetle. Surely, he could be considered very dull and inadequate in the assessments of his other insect friends. Overhead, he observes the beautiful butterflies and the glorious dragonflies, but the caterpillar can only crawl about on his many legs. Never mind that I painted him in such a way to keep him safe from predators, preserving him for a greater glory. From the caterpillar's view, his life is worthless and he is devoid of beauty. The only thing he can do is crawl and eat and eat and eat. How boring that must seem to him! Every few days, he grows too big for his skin, so he walks out of the old skin to expose a new, bigger version of himself. Then, one day, he finds something arising out of his little body that causes him to adhere to a stem or to a twig. His latest version of skin begins to create a cave in which he can conceal himself from the world. For a while, the chrysalis cave is comfortable. He can rest and eat without the fear of being eaten. There is no longer a desire to crawl about. He is content to stay in this hiding place. However, his situation does not remain static. Something very odd begins to happen as he rests and feeds. All that he has known of his inner body begins to dissolve. Special little spots, once hidden within his former caterpillar body, now begin to transform. A new body structure has replaced the old. He begins to grow a new head, a new mouth, long legs, and wings. Now his body feels a burning sensation and his legs ache. He begins to wonder if he will die in this painful, entrapped, condition. The former little caterpillar begins to feel totally out of place as fear creeps into his heart. "Who am I?" he wonders? "Why is this happening to me?" But before he has time to consider his questions, he begins to feel as if he will suffocate. The casing around him is now pressed tightly against his body. His legs and neck feel cramped. He has the urge to stretch out, but he can't within that tight space. In a near panicked state, the caterpillar begins to push, and to kick against his paper dwelling. He tears at it with his mouth and thrashes until the chrysalis breaks open. Where crawling was once a natural movement, it is no longer an exercise of ease. He is weak. His new wings are wet and collapsed. His long legs are nearly useless, except for anchoring and clinging to the branch. After fighting to emerge from the chrysalis, he must now use his energy and strength to push fluid from his belly into his wings, so that they might expand. Now is the time for great faith and for great patience. He must hang upside-down to dry and to slowly spread his wings. Then, in just the right moment, the new butterfly drops down to stand upon his feet. He flaps his wings and flies. Now a creation of beautiful coloration … one who can flutter above the earth below … the butterfly has a whole new perspective of who he really is. Everything in his life, up until now, has been preparation through challenge and struggle. Now there is freedom for him, and a new understanding of his created purpose. My desire is that as each of you, as you live out your life, will undergo a complete metamorphosis, which will take you from earthbound carnality to Kingdom flight.

Do you recognize your own experiences, perceptions, struggles, and transformations being reflected in the life of the butterfly, little ones? You cannot grasp the fullness of the Divine masterpiece, contained in your own life nor the necessity of the process that I have established to fulfill your destiny, while you are still a caterpillar … while you are still being transformed.

You don't understand the importance of developing humility, as you crawl about taking on food in the Spirit, while still lacking your true wings. Pride will allow you to be devoured by the enemy. It will stunt your development, so that you will never fly for Me. Dining on My Word is an absolute necessity, if you are to have a foundation that will enable you to grow in wholeness and in truth. Do not despise the days of humble, boring, beginnings. Do not compare your process and your level of endowments to others, who may be beyond you in the journey. These 'high flyers,' if they truly are of Me, have gone through the same process in which you now find yourself. It is a step by step process … always shedding off the old nature, and the immature constructs, in order to fit into the new learning adventures and understanding that I will bring to you along the way. If a caterpillar did not shed his old skin, he would die, being crushed by the confinement around him that would forbid his growth into the new thing.

When you feel confined … when you feel as if you need to break out … make sure that it is MY process that is calling you to emerge. My enemy will cause an evil swelling of pride and offense … of jealousy and discontentment … to puff you up, so that you will break out and grow into his wicked form, or die in the process. Resist the pride of offense. Reject the fires of deception and assumption. Quench the burning desires that arise from insult or impulse. Such things are intended to form the hot steam of anger within you. That steam will cause you to feel a pressure, demanding that you breakout. What you abandon, in that escape from pressure applied by the enemy, will not take you into My fulfilled destiny for you. When you are in discomfort, feeling contained and restricted, seek My counsel regarding the source of that distress. Do not assume that the pressure is holy nor that the breakout desire will take you to a positive, Kingdom level. It may be the opposite. Find out what I am doing within you. Yield only to My processes. Allow ME to split open what confines you, as I lead you into a new level of development toward your completed destiny. Only then will you be provided with a new, secure covering that will usher you into the next stage of your life's journey.

When you are about to go through a marvelous transformation of thinking, behaving, speaking, or understanding, I will hide you away ... even isolate you for a time. You may feel the sting of persecution and misunderstanding impacting your heart. Betrayal, lies, and acts of cruelty may be attacking who you are in Me. I may have chosen to allow some of these painful events to serve as that which stimulates your soul to attach yourself to Me alone. As you withdraw in pain, hopefully hiding yourself in Me, it may feel as if your inner being is dissolving during this time of metamorphosis. You will feel weak and alone, so that you will hear My voice only and receive the comfort of My embrace above all others. You may feel confused, as the things and the people in whom you held confidence will abandon you. This is the great pain innate to the Garden of Gethsemane challenge of surrender. I will be with you in that pain and agony, walking you through to the glory that awaits on the other side of your chrysalis time. Honestly pour out your heart to Me, in the midst of your agony and aloneness. Where others would not care for your heart ... where others could not relate to your pain, suggesting that it is nothing to be concerned about ... I will hold your heart closely to mine. I know what it is like to feel that same pain and to be stripped. I know the shame that wickedly empowered falsehoods try to shout into your mind. In My time of testing, I had the benefit of knowing, in advance, what would be accomplished by My suffering. But you, littles ones, must trust solely in My goodness and in My love for you. I am not cruel nor uncaring. I want only what is best for you ... that which will make you strong and effective as truth bearers in a world at war against My truth.

In your time of agonizing transformation, I will be growing long legs in you that will enable you to stand higher above the ground, rather than crawling upon it. I will be developing strong wings in you, so that you will soar in grace and beauty. Where before, you could only munch on solids, I will now

THE CRY of the SHEPHERD

enable you to drink from the nectars of heaven. Your mouth will be transformed to accommodate the acquisition of this newly available spiritual food. Your head will be transformed into a renewed mind to hold and to carry the revelations of wisdom and truth. You will become My agents of spiritual fertility: enabling new fruit to form where there has been barrenness. Even as a butterfly carries pollen from flower to flower, enabling fruit to form, I will take you from place to place, and from person to person, to transmit the truth that you will gather from Me as you journey. You are to initiate much holy, enduring fruit by the life you live for Me.

When the moment arrives for you to exit your chrysalis time, you will have to work your way out of confinement. By that, I mean you will need to choose to emerge… to embrace the new thing I have established for you. It won't be easy at times. Your new abilities will be strengthened and tested as you battle to move out into a new day. All that effort that will be exerted is part of the process I have chosen for you. You may emerge into a brighter light but then be surprised at how weak you are. Your wings will be wet and limp. Give yourself time to hang in an upside-down world for a while, until the gifting that I have deposited into your belly presses out to inflate your wings. Test those wings a bit before you try to fly. Exercise your faith and find rest by giving Me praise. Spread those wings, and then move them according to the leading of My Spirit. In My perfect timing, you will lift off and begin to fly. Your beauty will be visible to many.

Some of those witnesses will be filled with joy on behalf of what I am able to do with you in this new state of being. Others, who are still earth-bound in soul, will look at you with a jealous eye. Some will try to declare you as a fraud, insisting that you are really nothing more than a caterpillar wearing butterfly garments. Ignore their charges and simply fly.

Attend to the assignments I give to you.

Now, hear from Me, little butterflies, as I share a few things that you need to keep in mind concerning your Kingdom state. Butterflies are never pests to those who love and appreciate the beauty of My Kingdom. You are meant to be a blessing to Me, and to this world. Butterflies never sting and they never bite. Butterflies are creatures of the daytime … of the light. You are not to be like the hairy, colorless, moths, whose hearts prefers darkness as they are drawn to a futile, false light. Moths become the prey of the bats that fly at night, while you remain safe in Me amid the darkness. Butterflies know that they did not create their own beauty, and, thus, they give Me the credit for the glory that shines from them. They are creatures without pride, as you also must be. In their transformed state, they never look backward, longing for caterpillar days and experiences. They know where they came from. They remember the struggles, so that they will have compassion when they see the chrysalis of another butterfly going through metamorphosis. When a newly emerging butterfly appears, you will note that mature butterflies will flutter about, encouraging the weak and wet brother or sister to be patient with the process. Often, they will perch nearby to flutter their wings, creating a breeze in the Spirit, to aid the drying process. What they will not do, is to see an opening chrysalis, and then rush to help tear open the enclosure. If My natural order is not allowed to take place … a necessary order of events that builds strength and wholeness … the emerging butterfly will be damaged and never be able to fly. He will soon die.

A butterfly is not without enemies and predators, but it is far safer because of its ability to fly above the threats which are innate to ground dwellers. Their lives may be short, but butterfly lives are rich with beauty, grace, purpose, and glory.

What do butterflies bring to My troubled human children? What purpose do they serve? You can see these little messengers of Mine in the remotest places of the earth. They are a sign of hope and a reminder of resurrection. They are proof that the struggle is worth the pain in the fulfillment of divine destiny. Butterflies are meant to remind you that I am the One who transforms ugliness into beauty and weakness into strength. They speak to you the truth that life is a process. If you yield to that process, you will arise to heights that you never imagined. If you live as a butterfly, you will live as one, whose life has been transformed by a Divine hand. The pain that you will have experienced will be seen as having had purpose, to the point that you will look back and praise Me for allowing it. As you live out your life in this way, you, and the little insects whose life processes you share, will bring amazing joy and delight to My heart and eternal fruit grown from My gardens of humanity.

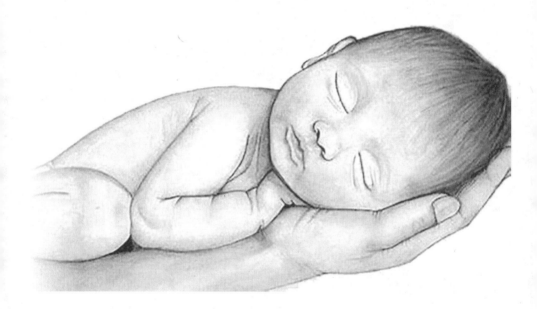

THE POWER OF CONTENTMENT

Little ones, perhaps one of the most powerful weapons of victory over your great enemy is the weapon of Contentment. Contentment is like chain mail around your soul, but, more than that, it is accompanied by Peace, which creates an impenetrable covering under that protective armor. Against these two, the enemy cannot prevail. Knowing this truth, he works constantly to drive you away from any element of contentment concerning your life.

First, let me clarify something at the very beginning of this time of sharing. The contentment, of which I speak, does not necessarily arise from accepting many of the things going on around you in the world. Injustice, unrighteousness, cruelty, hatred, and the like, must never be allowed to rest peacefully in your soul. The condition of the sinful world must not be regarded with contentment by your heart or mind. My Kingdom, dwelling within you, is to be your contentment. Many troubling things occurring in the lives of others …

whether arising out of the demonic or out of the thoughts and choices of human flesh … are not occasions for you to offer acceptance or to impart a blessing through your endorsement. I do not want you to be contented with immorality and perversion, nor with the slaughter of the innocent. I never want you to be content with credibility and power being given to lies. Instead, the personal contentment, of which I speak, solely arises from completely accepting and embracing that which I choose to bring into your life, or to give to you personally. What are these things?

For example: Out of an infinite number of options, I chose for you to have the physical appearance you now see in the mirror. Certainly, it is possible for your physical appearance to present the evidence of the challenges you have faced in life. Your visage also reflects the passing of years of the lifetime which I have granted you. Though you may disapprove of what you see, I delight in the way you have been created and in the way you appear to Me. The physical choices concerning your design … elements which I determined at the time of your creation … are good things in My eyes. I want you to be content with my artwork as well, rather than coveting the appearance of someone else. Your height, your nose structure, your racial lineage, etc. are all things that I have determined for you. I want you to rejoice in the features that have been created uniquely for you. The set time of your birth, and the time determined to mark the completion of your life, are ordained by Me. Be content with My choices. Perhaps most especially, I want you to be at peace with how My hand is moving upon your life, whether in comfort or in distress. You may have unfulfilled dreams, which cause you distress. I want you to surrender these things into My hand, lest they become a source of sadness or discontentment to your soul. If you hold onto a plan which I did not create … a dream of your making which has been frustrated because of My higher plan being in effect … you will not only become bitter in your disappointment, but you will reject the living plan for fulfillment that I am unfolding before you. What I offer, you will often reject because of the discontentment in your soul regarding the things of your flesh, which you are seeking above My higher plan.

Oh, how I long for you to rest in a state of contented trust concerning the details … the unfolding events … in your life that I have ordained! I never sleep, I am never inattentive, and I am never arbitrary. Well in advance of the appearance of any painful development or crisis in your life, I have seen the choices that you and others would make to bring forth the various distressing, and dangerous, developments in your life journey. The freedom, which I gave you to choose Me and My way or not, … this same choice that I gave all of my human creation at the beginning … I would never remove, even though I could see in advance the suffering that would come through wicked affiliations and rebellious choices. I am true to My word. I will not violate My decrees. In pain, I have watched the suffering caused by human sin. All the while, I have continually created opportunities of redemption and blessing to meet every wrong, foolish, or hurtful choice. With each wrongful choice that you make, I offer you an opportunity to change your course, so that you can securely come back to My path and to My divine order, which will prosper your wholeness, safety, and destiny. Sometimes the way I choose, for the redemption of your foolishness, brings a chastening of your flesh. So often, you rail against this choice of My wisdom. In my love, I allow the consequences of your sin to discomfort your life, so that you will become keenly aware of the high cost of rebellion … so that you will come to understand that you have chosen wrongly and foolishly. At other times, I will allow the fruit of your rebellion to present a visible lesson for others to consider. Rebellious children often need to behold a warning, or to be given a reminder, to grasp the truth regarding the consequence that will arise from their sin against Me and against My order.

Still at other times, I will allow you to feel the sting, and to endure the pain, that comes from others rejecting My message delivered through you. It may seem like a great injustice that I would allow you to bear the pain of another person's sin, arising from an incident when you have acted righteously and obediently. In that moment, it is My choice for you to become a suffering servant for My purposes, so that another one, whom I love, can realize the price that their own sin brings into the lives of others. Will you bear this injustice, if it comes to you as a choice from My hand? Will you trust Me to add richness and blessing to your life … even expanding you in authority, wisdom, and in growth … as a result of putting you through such a trial? My servant, Joseph, was willing to bear great injustices so that others might know of My truth, My ways, and My love.

So often, My children cry out in angry confusion, railing against Me when they feel intense pain. They do not understand why a loving Shepherd has afforded such suffering to them. Discontentment and anger can arise quickly in a soul which does not trust My wisdom, and My love, in such matters. Many have accounted Me as cruel and unfaithful. Some have turned away from Me for a time to lick their wounds, rather than coming to Me to rest upon My heart where they would receive healing and truth in the matter. They become full of discontent, which often turns to bitterness and willfulness, as they reject My choice. Rather than turning to hear My heart, and to receive My divine support until the test is passed, they quickly turn to their own understanding. They run to other human beings to justify themselves or to find comfort. Their personal 'wants' assume a higher value than the option of accepting the choices which I would make on their behalf. The treasures that await them, from the process of overcoming and from the experience of returning to Me, never come into their lives. The joy of such things is never realized in their hearts. The experience of abounding victory, built into every presenting challenge, slips away, when discontentment rejects an acceptance of My perfect will for them.

Little ones, would you be content in My will if I would leave all your worldly aspirations unmet in order that My eternal aspirations for you, and through you, could be satisfied to a greater level of Kingdom gain and glory? Would you be content to abide alone, with Me as your Beloved and Champion, rather than having a human spouse? Would you allow Me the honor of bringing to your arms an abundance of spiritual children, who would accompany you into My eternal Kingdom, rather than giving you your own physical children to embrace? Would you allow Me to remove all your material wealth so that I could place in your hands immense, eternal wealth, that will never be lacking or depleted?

Allow Me to explore these questions even more deeply with you. Would you be willing for Me to allow you to remain in physical blindness, rather than restoring damaged eyes, if to remain physically blind would increase your spiritual sight? Would you be content in this circumstance, which the world would deem to be a tragic loss? Would you be willing to have a loved one come home to Me, to abide in My glory, accomplishing a greater thing, rather than having your prayers for healing be answered? Would you be content with that … with knowing that a promised eternity awaits you together … knowing that your loved one has been honored with receiving a gift of beauty and rest beyond your imagination?

Rather than removing you from the path of a great threat, would you be content to go through the storm or to face the attacker, if I chose that for you? And would you be content to be cut off from all that is dear to you, if such isolation would serve My divine purposes? Such things are opportunities that I give to My chosen ones, so that they can know My heart more intimately and come into a deeper fellowship with Me. Be assured, that every pain you feel, or have felt, is also an experienced pain for Me, personally. In truth, I have absorbed the greater portion, even though, at the time of suffering, you may not be able to embrace that as truth.

Ahhh, little ones! How precious you are to Me! How precious your heart is to Mine! I know that I ask things that may be difficult for your flesh to accept. And yet, I have given you the powerful Spirit of My truth to abide within you. Your spirit can leap to embrace My choices for you … even the most painful ones … if only You turn to Me at the first sign of challenge, pain, or loss. Arise to embrace that Spirit of Truth, to interpret the course, and to bear the demands of the presenting challenge. Holding tightly to that which is eternal, and releasing that which is temporal, is the critical way to remain in a state of contentment. The chain mail, and the protective ephod of peace underneath it, will protect your heart from the blade of the enemy. The helmet of salvation will cover your mind against the blows of assault. My truth will gird up your loins, and My Word will guard your feet against the thorns. The experience of war may come without warning. The storm and tempests may rock your little boat upon the great sea of life, but the one who rests in contentment, concerning My choices in the moment, will emerge intact of heart and victorious in spirit. Whether your body weathers the storm, emerging beyond the test, or whether I call for your spirit to fly back into My eternal presence, the peace will remain. You will remain unmoved, while My enemy must then change his course as a result of the defeat you have delivered to him. Therein lies your victory over him.

Do not be afraid of that, which you cannot see nor understand, precious ones! I AM the One who carefully holds and securely keeps the life you have given into My hands… a life intended to live under My complete sovereignty. Through your life, lived in contentment, blessed with trust, and operating in unity with My purposes, others will discover that the peace radiating from your soul is contagious. It will radiate through the heavenly realm; joining with the unending abundance found there. Its reflection will shine upon the earth, bringing an example of eternal victory in the present day. All will be well and in order, even though, to the world, it will not appear to be so. Those who seek peace will see it in you and will find it in Me because of your surrendered testimony. Then, little ones, your victory, acquired through contentment, will expand to encompass the lives of many. Come, have your mind and heart renewed! Let go! Fear not! Trust! Know My goodness and My faithfulness! You honor Me in your total submission to My wise choices. In turn, I honor you with an unquenchable light and with a transferable, transforming, peace, which will impact thousands. Through your contented submission to My way, will, and Word, the enemy will be sent howling into the darkness, absorbed in the agony of his defeat. How is that possible? It is MY CHOICE, My authority, and My delight to make this your reality!

LIVING INSIDE OUT

Precious little ones, how shall I help you live in power through these difficult days? So much of what you need to know is opposite from what your own flesh would tell you, and opposite of what is natural to your own mind. Come, let Me breathe upon you. Allow My breath to blow across your soul the new abilities you need to receive and the new understanding you must absorb to receive what now are only mysteries to you.

You have been taught to live in a protected and guarded manner. Your soul has built up a wall around itself behind which its precious contents are hidden from most people. You have been convinced that these things are priceless pearls to be kept far from the trampling swine. But I tell you this is a misapplication of those words directed to those who are members of My flock.

The pearls are of the Spirit, not the creation of the soul. I call for a different way of living— so that the gold I have refined in you is visible, and so that the ugliness that needs to be cut away is openly exposed in the safety of the flock. Herein lies the problem.

Over your length of days upon the earth, you have experienced the cruelty of unforgiving hearts, actions of betrayal, and words of punishing judgment to wound your soul. You have learned, and you have been told by those who count themselves as wise, to guard your own heart and mind so that the deeper things in you are kept safe. Surely, a severe attack on your soul can leave you with the sense that your life could end in despair if it ever happened again. You self-protect. It is good to keep your heart and mind under a guard, but that guard is to be Me, not your own self-protection. Apart from Me, you have no safeguard. The methods your soul applies to keep you safe actually put you at more risk. The protected darkness of the soul, that seems to be treasure, gives a place for My enemy to deceive you all the more. The good things of your soul become hidden by the dark things that need to be excised. Because of this, the deep treasure in you can be hidden from others, while establishing the soul in a position of self-idolatry. Let Me explain.

When someone once declared lies about your words, actions, or intentions, what was your first inclination? Was it not to explain passionately, so that your truth could be heard and accepted to quench the misinformation? Perhaps you trusted someone and allowed that person to come in closely to embrace the deep things of your soul. You did not hold back in loving or in sharing. The bonds of kinship and trust seemed to be unbreakable. But then the unthinkable happened. Your weaknesses were reported to others or thrown up in your face. Your human frailty was accused. Your strength was declared to be a self-established imposter. After the weeping passed, the soul worked quickly to repair the damage. Vows were made against future trust. Anger sent the offender far away. Accusation and self-justification merged to form an offensive weapon of power to invalidate the one who had attacked you. As a guard for your heart in the future, you were kept on watch for any hint of similar patterns in those yet to find a place in your heart. At the slightest hint of similarity, you applied the reality of the past pain to the new relationship. You moved ahead of any potential offense, applying the experience of the historical relationship, and the response to the pain you once felt, to this unrelated situation. In doing so, you not only declared death over a new and precious thing, but you gave continued power to past sin. Are these things not true? The wrong message you have received is that the soul must survive at all costs. Supportive comrades will tell you that the richest part of your being ... your heart, your mind, or your will ... has been violated. Is this truth as I declare it? No.

In My Kingdom, there is a different order and a different reality. The deepest interior of your being is your spirit which abides in My presence. This portion of you, which has gone from death to life while you still walk upon the earth, now abides in the deepest level of truth. It contains the deepest treasures of your being. Does this truth cheapen or discount the soul? No. It puts it into perspective. Does this suggest that it is acceptable to abuse the soul or the body? No. It only put the priority of value into order. Every facet of My human creation is of deep value, but the portion of highest treasure is the spirit. It is in the spirit where love and truth infuse My human creation. It is here where revelation bursts forth to correct the errors of the soul and to discipline the self-indulgent body. It is the power of the spirit that enlivens both the dying soul and the weary physique. It is the spirit where the true power abides to defeat every attack of My enemy. Why is this so poorly understood among My flock?

The way of the world is to exalt the body and the soul. It seeks to immortalize the endowments of the soul. Human wisdom is exalted. Human feelings are worshipped and served. The human will is seen as the ultimate power to demonstrate and to achieve power. If those who walk upon the earth have been born only of the earth, this is all that they can understand. However, the members of My flock are born from above the earth in My Kingdom. Shouldn't they now exhibit a different reality from those whose perspective can only be carnal? This is My desire and My longing.

Consider those who are not of My flock, but who claim a higher enlightenment from another spiritual realm. These seek to give evidence that mind, will, and emotions abide in perfect peace as they transcend the challenges of the earth. These, too, seek after the power of the spirit, but the place from which their spirit draws information and power is not Me. These enlightened ones deny the realities of the true human condition as they replace them with delusions. The delusions do not come from My Kingdom, for I am all truth. These disciples of transcendence actually deny truth rather than embrace it. If their false truth and if their power is not of My Kingdom, from where does it come? The vulnerability of the human soul has been exposed. In feeling helpless to understand and to cope with the confusing pain of the world, these have used their soul power, in concert with unholy spiritual delusions, to create a reality that is only paper, bells' sounds, and smoke. Their truth is as sand that can be washed away in a heavy rain. If they would come out of their need for comfort in their quest of truth, and be willing to look at the pain of truth, they would find it. The painful reality is that the human being is in a fallen state from which it can never be raised except by the blood I have shed to redeem it.

You may not have intentionally exalted the soul over the

spirit, but surely you have done this. How can such a condition be changed? The first step is to embrace the reality that the deepest treasure within you is found in your spirit as it communes with Mine. This is the reality that I want the world to see and to experience from you. If your priority is for those around you to see and to admire your abilities of the soul, and to honor these things, the true riches within you will be left unseen. You will be left battling one soul against another, while neglecting the true warfare that is operating in the spiritual plane. Because of this neglect, your soul will be challenged all the more, as wicked spiritual forces have access to influence your soul and the souls of those around you. You will dwell in middle earth rather than in My Kingdom's power while you live out your life. The divine messages of truth that I have imparted to your spirit will remain silent and unshared. Eyes of admiration may rest upon you, but there will be no Kingdom fruit from you. You may acquire a position of authority among the flock, but you will lack position and authority in My Kingdom. Do you understand the seriousness of this?

As members of My flock, called by My name, you are to live your lives inside out. By that, I mean to say you are to present to others, foremost, the realities of your spirit and of My Spirit in communion with yours. Where the world admires the physical body as first priority and treasure, followed by the mind, will, and emotions as the second, you are to have a reverse order.

To My Kingdom dweller, the physical body has the least priority, the soul has the second priority, and the spirit holds the position of highest priority. That will cause you to be inside out from the world. My truth must be the presentation of your wisdom, rather than your own thoughts. My heart must be the operative expression of your emotions over and above the manifestations of your own carnal heart. The power of

My will must be the obedience of your actions, in superiority over your own will. Are you beginning to understand this?

Not only do I call you to live inside out, but I call you to live genuinely this way. It is possible to give others the impression that you are living out of My priority, while you are continuing to prosper your own position and power. The world of religion is filled with this falsehood. To live in this way is to be as a sea cucumber. This little animal is filled with fluid. When a threat approaches, he can easily turn himself inside out, allowing his contents to gush forth, giving the impression of self-death. When the threat passes, he can again correct his inverted posture and again begin to fill himself with water. Soon he will be as he was, having lost nothing, while gaining the power to continue to live on as he was. Likewise, those ingenuous ones, who are in My flock, can profess to be living out a sacrificial, holy priority. When challenged, they can turn themselves inside out, revealing what appears to be the willingness to die to self, filled with flowing water, in order to give a good testimony of themselves. When the questioner or the threat passes on, convinced that the priority is genuine, the sheep can again revert to the true form of his or her priority to continue on, the ruse undetected. Such living is an offense to Me and a mockery of My example to you. When you live in true Kingdom priority and live out of your spirit in communion with Mine, there will be true Kingdom fruit. When you are challenged and gutted by a threat, the contents of blood will pour forth ... My blood mingled with your own blood of suffering servanthood. The death in you is real, because the life in you is really Me.

It's time to stop living out of physical and out of soul priorities. It is time to live inside out in all things. You must stop investing your time in coddling your emotions back to comfort, when feeling hurt or afraid, and instead begin drawing from

My Spirit to obtain your comfort. It is time to stop expounding your understanding and preaching your own thoughts as wisdom, and, instead, begin to repeat the wisdom that you hear in your spirit from My Spirit. It is time that you cease trying to assert the power of your own will to control and to direct outcomes to benefit your own soul, and, instead, submit to My will that is spoken to your spirit for the benefit of My Kingdom.

The fruit of living inside out is not only that your being will be put into proper, created order, but that My Kingdom realities will be seen and heard in you, coming from you. Your witness has been weak because you have lived out of your soul's priorities and out of the honor of your flesh. You have been heavily self-defended. In doing this, you have defended sin and honored your own carnal positions. Where is your testimony to truth? When your witness has been a testimony to your own wisdom and power, who has been able see Mine within you? With all the fortifications you have built around yourself to protect your soul from injury, how can the holy vulnerability that I require be possible? You are called to be transparent. What does that mean? Are you to live out of your soul, allowing everyone to openly see your fallen-ness? No. You are to live out of My Spirit, so that others, who do not know Me, can see your healed brokenness of soul. I do not want you to sport your sin before others so that they will find kinship with you, but to reveal your repentance and the fruit of that repentance.

If you live your life out of your spirit, which abides with Me, those around you will see Me more than they see you. Will they like what they see? Many will not. Those who have found comfort in their sin prefer not to experience the light of My revelation within you shining upon it. Those who like to be self-justified, feeling capable in the power of their soul priorities, will shun the Spirit, suggesting that the carnal fruit of their soul is meaningless in eternity. The members of My flock who are as sea cucumbers, filled with themselves, convincing others of their Kingdom credentials, will despise the heat of My Spirit in you that evaporates the false, exposing spiritual bankruptcy. At the same time, those who do not know Me, but who are seeking after truth and wholeness, will be drawn to you. These little ones are tired of the burdens of their own soul. They are weary of seeing others who idolize the soul while professing to be people of spiritual priority. The hypocrisy has sickened them as it has sickened Me. To those who are afflicted in soul and searching for true relief, your spiritual priority and transparency of redeemed soul will be both a respite and a joy. They will come to you and in doing so, they will discover Me. That is My cry for you. I long for you to be one who abides with Me and in Me, to the degree that you can speak, touch, see, hear and act out of My Spirit. There are those who say this is impossible to accomplish while wearing human flesh. No, it is not. Have I not said what I have done, you WILL do, and greater things as well? If I lived, moved, and spoke out of My communion with the Spirit, will you not be able to do this as well? Certainly, it is so.

I lived My life among you as One who was inside out. So also, must you live in this way, to serve Me well in these days. Remember, in My Kingdom everything is upside down from the things of the earth. Your soul, which abides between the earth and heaven, can live out of either realm at any time. Choose to live out of Kingdom reality. Choose to live inside out with your greatest priority being found in the Spirit. Living in this way … living inside out, opposite from the order that the world has assigned for the human being … you will change everything around you. The effect of those changes will, at times, be painful to your soul, and even to your body, but know this: You were created to live this way. From the beginning, you were to be in the form that is now inside out from the world. When the world is gone, you will be the only form of being that remains. All that is inside out from My kingdom will be gone, and you will again be as I intended. Soon, little ones … soon this will come. Avail yourselves NOW to the changes that must be made. Give yourself into My hands that I might help you reverse your current priorities of living. What you cannot do, I can do with you. Does it hurt to be turned inside out? Yes, it can be painful, but oh so glorious in the final accounting and in the days from now until the end! Come … allow Me to turn you inside out, so that My glory within your innermost being will be clearly seen even now.

SEE WITH MY EYES

When you behold another one of my children, what do you see? Do you see the size of that human body? Do you see the age or the color of the skin? Do you notice the clothing or the cleanliness at your first glance? Notice what you see first. It will announce to you the priority of your heart. Do you see that which is eternal, or that which is temporal?

What do you conclude at your first glance? When your eyes light upon one of my human creations, your mind and heart will analyze what you behold. What assumptions arise in your thoughts? What judgments? Is this formulation process so credible, and so automatic, that you immediately incorporate your conclusions, laying aside all other possibly contrary information, which you might obtain through deeper exploration or understanding?

I have told you that your eyes can be deceived and that your mind and heart can lead you into error. Yet, on a daily basis, you ignore that truth to form mindsets and evaluations out of flawed processes. An injury to your heart can carve away a piece of that heart, which would be vital for you to see and to understand real truth. Only I can heal a wounded heart and restore that piece which was excised through hurt and pain. If I am not allowed to replace that piece of your stricken heart, the enemy will come to insert his own piece to mimic that which was genuinely yours from Me. That defiled insert will cause your pain to continue through skewed understanding, causing you to inflict pain upon others around you. The longer that false piece abides with influence in your heart, the more difficult it will be to surrender it for replacement. The human heart is so well self-defended that it will fight to maintain the falsehoods, which are actually destroying it. Until the time of deliverance removes that falsehood, those lies will become powerful factors in how you perceive, feel, understand, and believe.

Your eyes are too big, little ones. They hold too much sway over what you conclude to be reality. You have entrusted your mind with too much power to conclude what is truth, when, in fact, the deepest realities can never be approached through the human mind. The arrogance of human flesh has existed since The Fall into rebellion. You need MY eyes to be the gateway to your mind and heart. You need eyes that are empowered by LOVE, rather than by SELF. You need eyes that are passionate for truth, rather than yearning for power and self-edification.

Your heart is a mixture … a patchwork of foreign pieces … filling in the blank spaces that pain and delusion have left within you as you managed your life and formed conclusions on your own. Give Me your heart for purification and for mending. Give Me your mind to be renewed in the truth that comes only from Me. I am all Truth. Let Me be your eyes that perceive the realities of your life, and of all those around you. Let Me be the interpreter of your history. Let Me be the Composer of the Masterpiece of your present and future life.

You will know that you have begun the rich process, of re-creation into a being of My truth and understanding when you can truly SEE another person. As you behold the face of another, a burst of truth will arise in your soul saying: 'My Father loves THIS ONE as much as He loves me.' That truth will appear as a delight to your heart, when My mind operates within you. If any element of comparison, of that person to yourself, arises, you will know that pieces of My heart are still missing from within you. The deceiver will still be operating on the false pieces he injected into your losses of heart. My holy surgery will be able to remove them, as you reject them as false— as you submit to MY truth about your life. My heart will come to replace what has been lost to you, once the counterfeit has been eliminated.

· You see, little ones, I love ALL my human creation without condition. As I AM Love, I cannot cease to love, even to My own hurt. However, FAVOR is a different thing than love. Favor is the outpouring of opportunity, blessing, and gifting, given to those who have been faithful to obey and to love, as an expression of their recognition of My love to them. Indeed, some of My human children are more highly favored than others, but none are loved less from the very beginning. You have a choice to know Me, even as you have a choice to follow My lead into truth and love. I can passionately love the choices you make, even as I can passionately hate those choices which will take you away from my embrace, or away from your destiny in Me. Yet, I cannot stop loving all of My children.

So many of your choices begin with your eyes, imparting information which becomes the raw substance for conclusions in your mind and in your heart. Ask Me to give you My eyes, through which you will perceive the people and the circumstances in your life. Ask for My wisdom in truth to help you conclude rightly. See those with whom you live as I see them. With each passing person, and with each sojourner on the road of your life, declare: 'My Father loves this human being … this precious creation of human life … as much as He loves me.' Then, leave the matters of favor in My hands, rather than touching them with your own, clouded, soul, lest you become jealous and bitter in the comparison. In this way, My love within you shall arise, even as My peace … My SHALOM … shall flow through you as a rising river. When your time to live upon this earth comes to a conclusion, that river of life shall find its end at My throne, where you will enter into eternal love and peace in My presence forever. There, your eyes, your mind, and your heart will be forever healed. There, My truth will be fully known and completely understood, to the full capacity of your eternal being. This is My vision for you. Will you see it as well? Will you embrace it even now, my beloved? I wait. I love. I see you fully. Here are My eyes for you to use. Come!

PERFECT BALANCE

Little ones, what is the definition of balance? Is it equilibrium? Is it steadiness and poise? Is it being level so that things stay where you place them or so that all things are equal? Is it a matter of symmetry? Balance can be described by all of these things. However, I want to speak to you about specific balance in your life, both as individuals and in community.

There is a determined plot that has been working fervently against you by the design of My enemy. If he cannot pull you from the ranks of those who choose to follow and to honor Me, he works steadfastly to pull you out of balance. If he cannot accomplish his goal of making you lose your individual footing, he works fervently to put you and your community into a state of disorder, so that you and it will crash down in dysfunction. Sadly, he is all too effective in prospering these strategies against you. For this reason, I need for you to sit with Me for this time, to consider now what I tell you concerning balance.

First, let us consider your personal life. You were created by My hand to be well- balanced in both your physical walk and in your spiritual journey upon the earth. Within your brain and within the depths of your ears, I implanted a guidance system to keep you upright whenever your feet would be required to walk upon uneven surfaces. You have a built-in sense that enables you to know and to correct your body position when these systems are functioning well. A tilt to one side can be quickly adjusted by making a slight correction of body position to the opposite direction.

As a child, many of you took curious delight in spinning around in one place, purposely to disrupt your balance. In delighted giggles, you would stop spinning and begin staggering around, bumping into objects, eventually tumbling to the ground. For a while, the world surrounding you would continue to spin as My repositioning system within you worked to make the necessary corrections, restoring balance. While spinning can be fun for a while, it soon becomes a torment if it continues unabated. You were never created to spin, little ones. You were designed to walk forward in a productive and meaningful journey. At the same time, I have known, since the moment of the first human fall, that your journey would also include many uneven roads for you to walk. Some of those roads would be perilous, requiring great strength and balance, wisdom and skill, beyond what you alone could attain.

For these times, I have placed within your hands and within your hearts the knowledge that you have One who will stabilize, lead, and establish you upon all the roads of challenge. Too often, My human creation has chosen its own abilities and understanding. At these times, My children also spin in place and fall down. Sometimes they grab on to others, or bump into them in their imbalance as they tumble, bringing a group of sojourners down with them. Every time this happens, I am grieved in heart. Foolish little ones, you think yourselves to be self-sufficient and work so hard to demonstrate that illusion to yourself, trying to convince others of it as well. Stop spinning around … stop walking by your own strength over uneven and unfamiliar ground. Your foolish pride impedes your own journey and proves to be a hazard in the journey of others. Just sit down and let Me make the adjustments. Allow Me to open up your heart and mind to renew and to uncover the revelation of Myself that I implanted there at the very beginning.

When My children have balance within them that is derived from Me, they can walk on very high places without falling. They can cross over raging rivers, stepping precisely on the rocks I have placed for them in the midst of the torrent. When everything around them shakes … when institutions fall and when relationships shatter in the test of solidarity with My truth … those who walk in My ability to balance them will not lose their footing, nor will they lose their place upon the journey. When the strong winds of demonic attack, deprivation, and adversity blow hard upon them, My children will be unmoved by the assaults. Their balance and their security are found in Me … in this reality they can neither be moved nor blown away.

How many of you, sitting at My feet right now considering these things, are having memories and emotions flooding your soul? You can remember occasions in the past or events in the present where you have fallen. Perhaps the sensation of spinning still keeps your walk unstable and your mind in confusion. You have tried to engage life on your own terms and through your own understanding. You made an attempt to demonstrate your abilities, but you jumped ahead to prove yourself, leaving Me behind. Your emotions became confused, while your thinking and your steps became ineffective or counterproductive. Are you staggering even now? Have you fallen or are you in the process of collapsing even now? Sit down, little ones. Sit down and confess that you have allowed yourself to be deceived by your own pride or by the seductions of My enemy. I will put things back into created order. You may have to journey through some painful consequences of your imbalance. You may have lost valuable time that will not be restored to you. You may have self-inspired wounds that need to be healed. You may have some repentant backtracking to do in order to learn the lessons. I will assist you as you turn to Me, but you must do what I declare is necessary for you to become balanced in Me again … so that the days still assigned to you will flourish with prosperity and with joy. In the process, I will require you to cry out to Me on behalf of all those who may have tumbled around you as a result of your imbalance. You may be required to put on the garments of humility to seek forgiveness from those you have knocked over, in addition to raising intercession on their behalf. I do not consider it a matter to be taken lightly when those out of balance bring others to a fall. You are to support each other on the journey of truth and faith in the way of My Kingdom.

Now, I call you to consider another plot of My enemy, very often applied against your balanced life. Rather than footing, this is an issue of interior and exterior balance. To illustrate this form, I want you to consider a single cell of the human body. Each cell has a cell wall, setting it apart as a unit. The cell wall has a significant responsibility in the function and in the survival of that cell. It is specifically designed to allow into the cell the nutrients and fluids to keep it functioning while allowing the wastes to escape, keeping it healthy. There must be a specific fluid balance inside the cell in relation to its external fluid level, so that the cell keeps its designed form. To change the salt levels can either cause the cell to shrivel or to explode, as it allows too much fluid in or too much to depart. There must be a perfect balance of life-giving elements on both sides of the cell wall.

How does this apply to you, little ones? Have you not read in My Word that the assembly of My followers is like a body? Have you not read that each part has a function which joins to another, creating organs and systems of life under the control of the Head? It is from this parable that I speak to you now. Each of you has been given the gift of free will to choose. Some of you choose well, while others struggle in using that gift wisely. Consider your free will to be your personal cell wall. I give you the ability of choice to select what you will allow into your thoughts, and those things which will be prospered through your actions and words. Many things come from My enemy with the intention of penetrating your cell wall. Images, desires, illusions, lusts, indulgences, emotions, lies … these are just a few of the things that satan would like to bring through your cell wall to be established in your being and demonstrated through your dysfunction. If he cannot cause you to abandon the journey with Me, he will try to implode you or to explode you by causing you to be out of balance. How?

So often, My little ones want to serve Me with all that they do. Truly, this is a great delight to My heart and a great honor to My name. It is a gift that I seek and which I cherish. The enemy knows this well. It is something that he despises. If possible, he will try to bring through that cell wall of free will a multitude of good things, making them seem like requirements established by Me. He adds to my Word his interpretation of what I desire and what pleases Me. This is called religion. He brings a list of rules and regulations that I have not established, but which seem like a good thing for My children to do as a way to raise their level of holiness. Soon, without consulting with Me, they put into practice many of his suggestions. The underlying intention is for My children to be seduced into prospering their own level of holiness and righteousness through observing man-made regulations. However, the intention is not to affect only the individual, but to cause that individual to build a rigid wall of rules and prideful conditions, setting himself apart from others. Rather than the interpretation of My Word and My commands being established by My Spirit, these things are formulated by oppressing spirits intending to shackle My little ones. As more and more assumptions are added about what I require and desire, and as a more rigid cell wall becomes established around that cell, the pressure builds internally. To protect what My children see as good and inviolate, the wall refuses to allow in any more revelation or Spirit. It does not see that much of what is retained inside is waste, bringing toxic effects to hearts and minds. What purpose … what life does it prosper in contributing to a healthy body? Its rigid cell wall looks more like a mere plant cell rather than of human substance and endowment. When these kinds of cells group together, you end up with something that represents wood … often dead wood. Over time, the cell majoring in legalistic input, but lacking in the output of toxins, can explode in ruin, as you have seen in many misguided religious cults. What I would desire to be life-giving has become lifeless, leading to ruin.

On the other hand, there is an opposite threat of imbalance. My enemy comes this time with many opportunities and needs to be met by the cell. He speaks that these are requirements … all of them … and that no one but this individual has the ability or the responsibility to accomplish these vital tasks. He speaks that the quality of life of all the other cells surrounding this one will be negatively impacted if this one cell neglects even one of these tasks. Again, often without consulting Me, this little one will set out, with the intention of honoring Me with his labors, on an assignment I have not established for him. He has no ability of himself and he lacks the understanding and the wisdom to recognize that truth. His heart is set on pleasing Me, while not being aware that only My enemy is pleased by his soulish labors. Over time, this little cell pours himself out FOR Me without it being OF Me. All the while, he has neglected taking in the refreshment and nourishment that is necessary. Rather than dining upon My food, he begins to devour his own strength and substance to continue his work … finding his joy in the act of accomplishment. Over time there is nothing left except a shriveled little cell with no life and no eternal fruit for his labor. I grieve that the free will was poured out with good intentions but which, in reality, prospered rebellion. Rebellion, you ask? Yes, rebellion. My voice in the matter was ignored and My Word was unintentionally set aside, allowing the soul to drive the life of My child, rather than it being led by My Spirit. Obedience is the opposite of rebellion. Self-determination is pride, while submission to My voice is true humility.

As I have shared these things with you, have you felt your heart being convicted? Know that in these things I feel compassion for My little ones in their well-intended activities, although they were done in deception. Quickly, I would bring them into balance. If My Spirit was allowed to be the gatekeeper of the cell wall, then things would remain in balance. If the human soul is allowed to be the gatekeeper, things can quickly fall into imbalance. Come to Me before you fall into a state of implosion or explosion. Allow Me to reorder that cell wall and to clean out the toxins … removing the rigidity of the deceptions. Allow Me to bring in the good nutrition and the wisdom to process it into life-giving endeavors.

"The cells of My body are to join together, allowing Me to establish organs and body systems to bring visible life and function to life in Me upon the earth. My Kingdom lives through this Body I have established and blessed.

Now, I must caution you concerning one more danger of imbalance. Beware of organs out of balance. Organs made of healthy cells functioning together are a glory to Me. I have differentiated the cells and individually placed them within the organs for full function in Me, so that the world will come to see Me in you. Too often, this is not the case within the individual fellowships of My children. Wherever there is My Spirit bringing life and unity of function in a body organ, My enemy will try to infuse that organ with the elements which will bring destruction.

Consider these things: every cell is meant to have a function in the organ. If any cells are forbidden to function or are set aside without being allowed to make a contribution, the organ will not grow. There will be stunting and immaturity. The organ will never come to full strength or glory for My Kingdom. If a few cells try to pick up all the work of the organ, it will soon become lopsided and then weakened. Balance and symmetry in the order means that ALL cells are empowered and released to function as they were created, placed and ordained by Me. In My wisdom, I gathered the cells together and I gifted them uniquely, so that there would be no lack.

Do you sense a lack in your fellowship? Are there some members enjoying the benefits of the environment, but not being allowed to contribute to the organ so that both it and they could grow? Are there leaders and members of the fellowship carrying the majority of the labor? Is there fatigue in your midst? Check your heart for any deception seeded in by My enemy. Have you heard that it is ALL up to you … that no one else is trustworthy, willing or able to share the load? Are you unwilling to share what you believe is yours alone to bear? Are there gifted ones you are waiting to release until you see them fit to be released? Ask Me for My determination of these things. Truly, in these days ahead, I will do surprising things that will offend your souls. I will ask you to trust Me with the work of the organ and allow Me to quickly empower the young cells and the formerly damaged ones which I will heal quickly. You will need faith, vision, and discernment as you have never had before. Every decision you make must have My input and My seal of approval to prosper the miraculous I intend to bring. I will tell you what changes to make as leaders and as vital members. You have work to do that will require ALL of you to be engaged in the work of the organ and the body.

Damaged cells form scar tissue if they are left unhealed. Release those I have empowered with healing gifts and do not surmise which ones are acceptable to Me for this job. I will tell you clearly. Rebellious cells, determining their own order of operation, will bring malignancy into the organ. Release into action those with gifts of discernment, deliverance, and teaching. Eject from the fellowship those that I tell you will not come into alignment with My way, will, and Word. Even as a virus or bacteria can infect an entire body to illness, so also can a plant of My enemy sent into your midst sicken and weaken you. Make no assumptions and reject all manipulations. Discern My voice and instruction to you each day.

Fear and pride are your worst enemies. One suggests that it is your job to protect and to accomplish all that which I have established through you. I, who have called you to this task, will do it within You. I will provide and I will protect. The other enemy suggests that no one other than you is properly equipped, steadfast, mature, or able to accomplish the work before you. This is a clear deception. You see with physical eyes too often, missing the provision I have placed in front of you.

If you are tired and discouraged … if your labors bring less joy than frustration … if you are unable to be at peace in your heart because of the pressure of your responsibility or because of the requirements you bear in serving Me … if you feel you are all alone in your service to Me … you are out of balance. My enemy has been working out his plan to knock you down, to explode you, or to implode you. If you remain in imbalance, you could become sick, little ones. Lay it all down at My feet, and place yourself in My hands. I will breathe upon you. I will reset your balance mechanisms created within you. I will squeeze the toxins out of you with My loving embrace. Your part is to ABIDE IN ME. Allow Me to fill you and to cleanse you. Allow me to interpret for you the realities around you from My perspective. Allow Me to heal you and to deliver you from the pride and fear, from the confusion, and from the diseases of soul that have weakened you. It is My plan and My desire for you to leap upon the high places with agility and with perfect accuracy. It is My plan and My desire for you to grow to your full dimensions as cells, as organs, and as My Body. As the world shifts into its greatest levels of imbalance and dysfunction, come into perfect balance in Me, little ones. From that empowered position you will stand with strength and wholeness, giving great glory to Me and great defeat to My enemy as the world stumbles and falls. From your position of perfect balance in the midst of great shaking, you will be able to reach out to grab hold of many, who, without your grasp, would be lost in an eternal fall.

ALL CREATURES
GREAT AND SMALL

Little ones, have you ever considered the sacrifices that the creatures in the animal kingdom offer to your world as a benefit for you? I have created them for My delight. I have created them to demonstrate My extravagant hand in designing beauty, variety, and function. I intend for you to see My love woven into their structures, even as My care for you is confirmed by their service. Some would say that certain members of the animal community appear to be the signature of My sense of humor to gladden your hearts. This is true. Each animal and each insect brings a service, a blessing, and message to you. Some are obvious, while others require close scrutiny and wisdom to glean forth the purpose embedded in their reality upon the earth. Consider a few of these truths with Me.

Some of the creatures are given to you to be your physical servants. The horse can carry you as well as a load that you would have to bear without him. Upon his back, you can pursue and overtake someone on foot. In a time of leisure, you may simply allow his speed to carry you to a place of delight as the wind blows through your hair— as the scenery changes around you. The ox can pull a plow, even as the strength of the horse is able. He, too, can carry a person or a large burden from one place to another. The great and mighty elephant can push over trees, out of which you may build a house or a bridge. As they snap off trees, a road of travel can be formed where only a forest once stood. Even the humble donkey is able to take the weight of a journey from your legs and feet. My animal creatures often serve to make your life and work load lighter. Without the help of mechanical devices, there are some tasks which you would not be able to achieve at all, if not for the service of My animals.

Many of the creatures I have placed upon the earth are now food for you. These animals sacrifice their blood and breath that you may eat and live out of their loss. This is part of My plan and therefore need not bring grief to your heart. The animals that I have chosen to sustain your life often have more than one gift to bring. The female clucking chicken, honking goose, and quacking duck offer their eggs as well as their own flesh for your consumption, while the males have little else to give. The cow and the female goat bring milk, cream, cheese, and butter to bless your table, before their own flesh is also served upon the platter. Most males have nothing to offer you short of their own lives as acceptable food, and the gift of their progeny. The fish has her eggs to offer you, but most often she must die for them to be accessible. There is nothing else that the male fish can offer to your stomach other than his own flesh. Nothing else but the total life can be given or harvested. I would not want you be casual concerning this gift to your life arising from sacrificial death. Surely, there is a message of a greater sacrifice spoken within it. Offering one's whole life, so that others might live upon the food of it, is a sacred gift to give. It demands the recipient of the feast to bring forth fruit in his or her life that will honor the sacrifice that supplied it.

The members of My animal creation also bring gifts to you of protection and of covering. The sheep has shared its wool so that the cold of winter nights would not harm you. The sheep is able to offer you this gift of covering and yet continue to live on. This is not true of all who clothe you. The leather made from cattle, pigs, crocodiles, and others allows your feet to have shoes, your trousers to have belts, and your shoulders to have a coat, for example. In this way, the body of an animal has been given to shield you, to adorn you or to bless you with clothing. The very covering of protection that I gave to them, they have now given to you in the time of their death. Have you ever snuggled underneath the warmth of a down-filled quilt, or rested your head upon a soft feather pillow? Have you been mindful that these things came to you through the death of a creature? I do not speak this for sadness to arise in your heart, so that you lay aside the comforts given to you by these sacrifices. These things are in My plan of blessing for you. Again, I want you to see the message embedded in these things. Whatever has been given to you for comfort and for protection is not for you alone. You must know that the gifts I have given to you for comfort and protection must eventually be passed on to others, gifting them. Some of your endowment you will offer while you live on, while other blessings may be given only by your death. I will speak more of this in a minute.

One last gift that I want to consider with you concerning My animal creatures is their service of comfort. Some of this comfort comes in the form of companionship to push back loneliness. Have you noticed the amount of love you receive and invest in your pet animals? The joyful bark and the wagging tail of your friend the dog, as he greets your return, can remove the frustration of a pressured work day. A purring cat affirms your presence in her life, while your stroke upon her fur settles down the noise within your own soul. The joyful sounds of the birds awaken you to a new day, announcing that the gift of life is still yours. When you are left alone to defend your home against the threat of a burglar, the sentry attention of the watchdog to every noise is a comfort to your fearful heart. I have given these animals a heart for you, and you a heart of love for them. The friendship between you and them is a gift from Me, but these furry and feathered friends must never become your priority over other humans, or over My Kingdom's work assigned to you.

So ... as I have given the creatures of the earth to feed you, to protect and cover you, and to comfort you, what is the application of these realities to your present spiritual journey? In these darkening days I want you to know that you, too, are given to each other, to present some of these things to each other, so that a powerful Kingdom prosperity can come forth against the darkness.

I call for each of you to help carry the load of the others. I designed for you to live together, individually before Me, but also in unified, sacrificial concert with each other for My purposes. In a time of spiritual war, this becomes even more vital. Some of you have been given a great capacity to bear suffering. When you meet one in the flock, who struggles to carry his or her burden of illness or loss, pick up what portion of these things I command you, through your service and strength, lifting these things from the one in struggle. This service may consist of bringing in food, cleaning a house, or enwrapping a weeping heart when trouble has turned someone's world into disorder. Weeping with one in pain lightens the load upon the heart of the other. When you come across one who needs help finding a way through the forest of confusion, walk with him or her, making a highway of truth as you strike down delusions. The strength of the whole flock increases as you share the load. The population of the flock increases as the world sees you do this service in love, and as it experiences personally your gifts of service.

The blessings with which I endowed you are not to be for yourself alone. If you have the gift of wisdom, you are to share it, feeding others who lack wisdom. If you have truth, you are to offer it up, at My command and in the way of My heart, so that the deceived can come out of the bondage of lies. This is bread and living water that I have placed within you for the purpose of feeding the starving. So be not afraid to offer it up. Do not ever fear being in lack if you live in obedience to My every command to pour out and to offer up. I am a never-ending supply. Noting that I, within you, am your provision and your life, you can offer yourself up and, in doing so, offer up Me to others, so that they, too, might live. Be careful, little ones. Note that you must not offer up yourself apart from Me, or without seeking My permission and form of service, or you will become depleted. If you are constantly feeding upon Me, you will always be able to feed as I direct you. If you turn away from My supply lines in order to create a line of supply of your own, you will quickly be unable to provide life for yourself or for others. Do not carelessly or arrogantly place yourself where your life is at risk. If the time comes, when I require your breath and blood on behalf of another, do not fear. This is the dearest form of love, and the greatest level of service to Me and to the others. Only I can call for such a sacrifice, and only I can prosper new life out of your death.

When you are in the midst of battle, My enemy will try to remove your cover. He will try to strip you of weaponry, of armor, and of fellow warriors. Do not allow him to draw near enough to grant him success. You must cover each other, keeping watch for any attack designed to strip the members of the flock. If someone's shield has been knocked away, stand offering the cover of yours until the shield of the other is replaced. If you find one, who has been wounded in the battle, offer the cover of your body, your weapons, and your strength until the medical team arrives to move him or her to safety and to healing. Be willing to be wounded for covering a dazed warrior, rather than running to your own safety. Your strength and gifting is not given for you alone, but so that you might fight together as a unit. Too often, My children become absorbed in their own challenges, to the point that they are blind to the needs of warriors around them. On the other hand, some have ignored My commands, staying behind, defending indefensible positions, in order to cover someone down in error. It would be better to cover the other, while pulling him or her to her feet, and commanding movement away from the current position. Unsanctified mercy is not blessed and honored by Me. Do not enable yourself or others to stay in weakness or in a position of rebellion, thinking that that this is your assignment. Forward movement and victory is My way. Obedience in bringing cover is what I require. When someone in the flock cannot hear what I am saying, repeat My orders loudly so that they can be heard throughout the ranks. To be silent may be to allow a number of warriors to wander unwittingly into the territory of the enemy. A fellowship of the ignorant is a hazard to the whole flock as well as to themselves. Battling without cover puts everyone at risk.

Finally, comfort each other. Even as the food I have placed within you is to feed others … even as the strength and endowments of gifting are intended to serve the others as you serve Me … so also is My comfort given to you to comfort others. When one in the flock is discouraged, be quick to encourage in the hope of My truth. When one is sickened and struggling against painful depletion, come underneath with the provision that I have given you. If one is seized with fear, aware that the enemy lurks nearby to kill and to steal, stand with him or her as a guard and as an assurance of My presence. Keep the enemy at bay as you employ My Word and the power of your arsenal of weapons given to you. Teach the untrained the ways of the war, and the use of the weapons so that they can arise in the comfort of My equipping. Many know and claim Me without knowing the ways of war … without acknowledging the power of the weapons … without submitting to My full authority to lead. These sheep stay confined in fearful places, attempting to defend themselves and what they possess, rather than advancing offensively against an aggressive enemy. Many of these shout orders of retreat and of false direction that put the flock into disarray. These things must stop.

Know that, in these days of battle, there will be losses. Some of My most select warriors will complete their assignments and will return to abide in My presence. This is not to speak of their failure, but of their success. Sadly, however, there will be many unnecessary and unproductive losses because the flock has not learned how to obey Me, nor how to serve each other. Do not be these sheep, little ones. Seek the lessons offered to you by the lives of My animal creation in this matter. I am not speaking of animal behaviors, but rather of animal service to your benefit. There are many more lessons to learn. Simply be in the posture of fulfilling your destiny in Me. Live obediently and sacrificially to the full extent that I created you. Allow Me to have all that you have to offer on behalf of others and on behalf of My Kingdom, and then watch the fruit that will arise from your life … and even from your death.

DEEP FIRE

Little ones, are you aware that under your feet, under the surface of the earth upon which you stand, there is a deep presence of great light, heat, and power? You walk upon the cool, top layer of the earth's skin, thinking that to be the secure reality of the earth's substance. Look below to the inner heart of the planet. There, you will find fiery magma in oceans and in rivers. This powerful substance exists in a constant flow, without your awareness. In a sudden instant, all the pride built upon the earth could be brought low by an eruption of this power upon the surface of your world. Likewise, there is an ever moving, ever powerful presence of My light, heat, and power in the spiritual plane that, when brought to the surface of the world, will change everything. It is time to put down your delusions of grandeur, little ones, for My reality is grand enough, and it is ever present, even if you are unaware of it. My hand is moving mightily. No one needs know the manner in which it moves. It is enough to know that it moves, most often unseen by human perception.

You seek to know the time … to know the day in which you are living. You seek to know the timing of the day of destruction, so that you might prepare and call others to preparation. I tell you this: the word has already been sent out, calling for preparations. The signs of the season have already been shown. Why, then, do so few heed the call? Why do they surmise that safety surrounds them, when all is in peril? Why do they count pennies, and store them away, when the value of their coins is about to be lost? Why do they move about in freedom, taking that very gift for granted? Truly, the days of free movement upon the earth are ending. The days of restriction and bondage, the days of imprisonment and isolation, are coming. What was seen as secure will be shaken. What was experienced as peace will become a sword of violence. What was understood as truth will be viewed as falsehood. Everything that can be shaken will be shaken. Only that which is rooted deeply in Me, and in My truth, shall endure. The compromises of men will be compromised. The wisdom of men will be shattered. My way shall stand.

When these things happen, what shall become of the light … My truth … in the world? Will it be lost? No. Will it be overshadowed? No. It shall appear to be disappearing, when, in reality, it will be going to deeper places. The light will be so scorned that it will become buried in the safety of surrendered hearts and lives. There, it will continue to burn with heat and with power without ever being snuffed out. This light of the truth will become more precious and more celebrated than ever before. For, when the darkness is darkest, the comfort of light becomes more precious. When a thing becomes scarce, infrequently seen, it becomes the substance of treasure. Its value increases when it is hard to find. Many people who will be groping for light … surrounded in darkness and walking in terror … will seek out My light within you.

In the deep places of your surrendered hearts, the light will change in intensity as it becomes more acutely focused and more tightly compacted. In this present day, the truth shines like a small candle in the world. In the darkest night yet to come, it shall become like a piercing laser. It shall cut, and it shall sear, and it shall have extraordinary abilities that have not yet been observed or experienced in the world. The light, heat, and power of truth are merely a lit match now. Then, they shall be as a reaction of fusion in the world.

Who shall be able to contain, guard, and use such light of My truth, and of My word? Truly, only those who can walk in surrendered obedience, without regard for their own lives, shall be able to do these things. Only those who can hear, know, and follow My voice … only those who will not shun My teaching … only those who are willing to die to their own ways and understanding … these alone will be able to claim the impossible. Only those who walk in humility and in love will be able to contain and to effectively use this light of My power. Only My children who know how to walk in humility and love can do these exploits of the extraordinary, which arise from handling holy fire. Those who seek to prepare for the days ahead must seek now for an anointing of these virtues. They need to lay aside all fear of their own exposure, and of their own burning flesh, that comes from dwelling in the light of My truth.

I placed the light, the heat, and the power of fire within the heart of the earth for them to have the ability to create and to recreate. I have placed My light, heat, and power of fire within you, little ones of My heart, so that you too can join Me in the process of creating and recreating in the days to come. Do not be afraid of the preparation that I bring to your soul and flesh. Do not fear the boastful roaring of the powers that dwell upon the earth as they threaten you with their unholy fire and with their perverted light of falsehood. Remember that My hand is always moving, under the surface, on behalf of those who love Me and on behalf of My purposes for creation. The heat of My holy fire, My light of truth, and My absolute power cannot be successfully contested by any challenger. As that same light, heat, and power abide within you, they also cannot be defeated. When challenged by unholy forces, this holy magma shall only go into a deeper place within you, to continue its movement until the moment I choose to bring it forth to transform the world. Soon, little ones … it shall be soon.

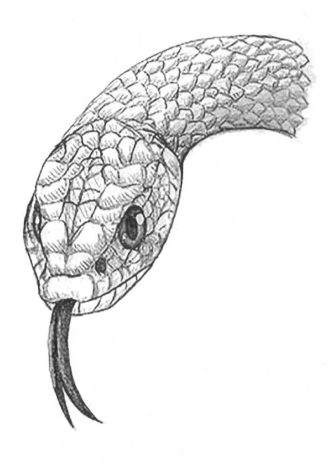

DEADLY DISTRACTIONS

What captures your attention, little ones? What is it that apprehends your thoughts, your focus, your heart … even your minutes and your hours? What is it that pulls you away from the essentials, while consuming your lives with the carnal irrelevant?

I have given you a life of extraordinary potential. I have entrusted you with a prescribed number of days to dwell upon the earth. Are your days prospering the fullness of your potential? Too often, I see My children treating the days of their life as a holiday when it comes to Kingdom realities and demands. Is it acceptable to take 'time off' from living the life of committed faith and of Kingdom responsibilities? The world is so enticing in your modern world. 'You deserve a break' is the message broadcast to human flesh. 'Make life easy and fun' is the mantra of popular culture. This, surely, is the assignment given to those laboring in the fields of technology and development. All the gadgets coming into the marketplace are intended to make life easier, more fun, and to facilitate a single mindset. What is that mindset? It is the idea that life is meant to be easy and to be enjoyed to the fullest extent of one's desires. These gadgets are no longer a supplemental accessory. They have now been promoted into the position of being an entitled human necessity. If the hearts of My children yield to the seductions of material fascinations, and of ideological posturing, where does that position Me in their priority, and in their assessment of what is vital and valuable? They have made Me irrelevant and outdated.

It grieves Me to see the lack of discernment in My little ones. They are so easily distracted by the technological fascinations created by My enemy. They recognize neither the source of these inventions, nor the negative impact these things are having on their priorities and on their time consumption. Is 'more' always better than less? Is 'fast' always better than deliberate? What empowers these digital distractions? That which empowers them has the ability to derail your mind, and to pervert your priorities, along with depleting your health and peace. Do you not perceive this? Little ones, while you are totally engaged with your gadgets and with senseless debates of intellectualism, the evil one is taking much ground from you.

What are you losing because of these distractions? First of all, you are losing precious moments, which are intended to bring forth wholeness, growth, and Kingdom expansion in your life. Relationships falter, and wane in significance, because of your time investment in THINGS. Hours pass by as you engage in mindless play, in net surfing, or in viewing television and videos. You grow mentally tired … even exhausted, without realizing the reason for that fatigue. You are being drained, rather than filled. I alone can fill you, but you have no time to attend to Me. Your emotions are unstable because of the stress that too much busyness and digital input places upon your soul.

While gaming activities can seem very exciting and challenging, they offer only emptiness when compared to what living life in the Kingdom will bring to you.

But gadgets, and their output, are not the only distractions that have captured your focus. Posturing for ascendency ... hours spent surmising about reality ... having endless discussions or arguments about the futile, miniscule, and erroneous also distract you from pursuing My Kingdom's truth and business. And how many hours do you spend being entertained by books that fail to grow you in wisdom and truth? Do you not see that this 'novel' entertainment subjugates your time and your soul? It fills you with fantasies and with misinformation about real life. Do you ever stop to think about the reality that what you feed your mind will birth its fruit in your spiritual journey and in your life? You get to decide what you will feed your soul. Will it be holy spirituality or carnality? You must choose the mind food and heart food that will make you more whole and more wise in order to be of service to Me in the coming battle. You will determine whether you dine on dead-wood and thus fill the cells in your brain with it, occupying the very space where My wisdom was intended to dwell. Has your consumption of mindless nonsense, and the emotional perversions of truth, become so automatic that you have failed to see that in each instance you are making a choice?

My enemy is filling your world with technology, with activities, and with philosophies ... in essence with empty input to keep you distracted from your destiny. He does this because he knows what fascinates you will become your investment. After being your investment, these distractions may become your focus, then your entitlement, then your necessity, and, finally, your priority. Sadly, these things can also become your passion, rather than ME. Where do you invest your time and your finances? What occupies the spare minutes and the free hours of your day? The world will tell you that you need to relax and to indulge your flesh. "After all, you earned it by working at your job."

Ah, little ones, I made provision for you to find rest away from your labors from the very beginning. It is called My Shabbat. The seventh day of your week is to be your time to rest and to delight in Me. What distracts you from taking that day apart from all the labors, amusements, and distractions? SATISFYING YOUR APPETITES … that is what keeps you engaged elsewhere! What is it for which you hunger and thirst? You have been deceived into thinking that you will find rest and joy in the sales that the shopping industry has established for the seventh day. The appetite for competition, and for sporting events, has consumed many Shabbats of My children. All these things prevent you from finding rest in wholeness. You wonder why you are so tired after your weekend. You may have had some extra time to relax, have fun, or sleep, but these things will never be able to give you what a few hours in My presence would give. How I long that you would hunger for ME … that your appetite for Me would consume you. I would so willingly fill you up with everything that you need or desire.

But there is one more thing that you must know about distractions, little ones. All the distractions, which are sent to engage your mind, will, emotions, and time, have an ultimate goal put into place by My enemy. He knows that when your focus is on the enticements of the soul, he will be able to advance his kingdom right under your nose. You will not take notice that the quality, the foundations, and the purpose of your life have been slipping away. Nor will you be aware of how lethargy, discontentment, perversions, and complacency have been settling in. While you are distracted, he will advance his troops with initiatives to steal the harvest and the peace from the earth.

In this season of the world, when I most need My warriors to be trained and engaged in battle, too many are sitting on the sidelines focused on satan's delightful delusions. Too many of you are weak and malnourished. You lack self-discipline and confidence in Me. You have neglected your training for spiritual war, but openly celebrate the victory of accomplishing a new level in your video game. All the while you are ignorant of the vital, preparatory teaching, which is contained in My Word. You turn away from My servants … those to whom I have given the wisdom to train you. When it's convenient, some of you attend to the Kingdom way, but then lay it aside when the distractions summon your attention. Foolish little ones, you do not realize that the enemy is already at the door? All of your pleasures and delights will vanish suddenly. There, you will stand, facing off with a powerful enemy, and being found totally unprepared. Even now, the dark kingdom has stolen great parcels of ground that were dedicated to Me by your forefathers. Are you even aware of it? More and more are being lost each day in the substance of your societal values, judgments, and practices. You cannot afford to lose more ground and yet expect to have a place to stand victoriously in righteousness. Your own self-righteousness will not qualify, neither will your excuses. The time of battle is at hand.

Little ones, I have great compassion for your weaknesses. I have great patience and overwhelming love for you. But, in urgency, I cry out to you now. Lay down the distractions. Turn away from the empty fascinations and seductions. Discipline your soul and take authority over your appetites. Return to My Sabbath and begin to find delight in your time with Me. Learn from Me, for My Spirit is a gentle teacher for eager students. Allow Me to cleanse you and to remove from you the addictions that have bound you. Renounce, reject, and repent all your unholy attitudes and behaviors. Unhook from the distractions that have held you captive. I will help you. There is no condemnation for your failures, but there will be no advancement in My Kingdom unless you make the change. You are too vulnerable unprepared and disarmed by My enemy. Rather than lose you, I may remove you into My safe habitation beyond this world.

Know that My great plans for your life are still intact. Some of those plans have been delayed in development, but they can be brought to fulfillment in the current moment very quickly, if you agree to make a change. And for those of you who have chosen the anesthetic of distractions to be the way to quench your fear regarding the future, know that I am totally in control of every aspect of the future. Those who walk with Me, and those who abide in My way, will be safe at all times.

You have now heard My urgent cry regarding this matter of distractions. How will you respond? Will you come away with Me, laying aside the things that entice you, and which occupy your focus, your finances, and your hours? I am here, eager to receive you. Your instructions, your weapons, your armor, your nutrition, and your rest are all here with Me, awaiting your commitment. Do not delay. Come away into the reality of My Kingdom and be prepared to fight for the spiritual high ground and for your heavenly homeland. The fulfillment of your destiny demands your choice.

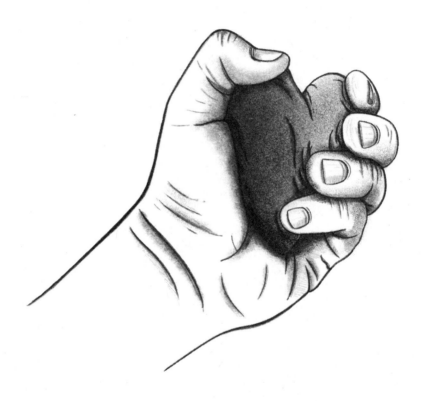

HEART CRUSHERS

Little ones, it is important for you to understand the ways of warfare, so that when it comes upon you, as it undoubtedly will come, you will be able to stand. Not only stand, but I long for you to advance against the enemy until victory is yours to claim openly. The battle the enemy chooses most often may be an attack on the mind, but his goal in this strategy is to seize the heart or to crush it. As we sit together, I will show you many things about the strategies and counter strategies of these battles. For right now, consider with Me the assault which has, as its goal, the crushing of the hearts of My beloved sheep.

Words have a great deal of power. The disorder of an amorphous idea can be sorted into understanding if there are words assigned to the concepts running across the mind. Feelings that are deep and overpowering … or perhaps emotions that are nothing more than a simple response to a current reality … are often hard to share with another person.

Words attached to interior feelings communicate those things that are intangible or poorly understood. Words … speech … language … these are gifts from Me. They were designed to bring order, fellowship, and understanding. Words are a way for the deeper part of you to be known by another person, whether you write those words or speak them. Words are meant to be based upon truth, giving truth a venue to be heard or read.

My sheep use their words freely … often too freely and too casually. Either they do not understand the power of their words, or they are insensitive in claiming their right to express them. Too often the words that emerge from My children are not words of truth, but rather they are words of deception built upon confusion, assumption, or presumption. Where words devoid of full truth are spoken, a process of destruction begins. Herein lies a key strategy of attack established by My enemy. Words that are not based in truth, but which are spoken or written into the lives of My little ones, become an attack on a heart through deceiving a mind.

The mind wants to know and to understand the realities of life. There is a sense of order in the person if the realities of life can be understood and managed. At one time, the minds of My children had the ability to embrace great truths, beyond what they can even begin to understand now. However, when the mind became carnal, it lost its ability to know and to understand things flawlessly. It also lost its ability to accurately build unseen concepts out of revealed truth. In spite of this lack, the human mind still tries to do things that, of itself, it has no way to accomplish. Since formulating reality from only portions of truth is a pattern of the fallen human mind, this same mind becomes an open doorway to deception. The Accuser comes in and out of that doorway constantly, bringing in deposits of deception … whether full deception or bits of falsehood mingled with a bit of truth … to plant seeds of destruction. It is here where the crushing of human hearts begins.

The first strategy in this planned attack is to embed falsehood within the mind of the individual about himself or herself. Whom does he use to speak his lies into the human mind? His primary tool is the mouth of those valued people in positions of influence or authority around one of My children. To a small child it is often the parents, siblings, or grandparents. To a student it may be a teacher or a spiritual leader. To a husband it may be a wife, or to a wife it may be a husband. Very often, the mouth used by the enemy to pass on falsehood is that of a trusted friend. In each case there is an attempt to alter truth to the mind … to pervert the reality of a human being created with divine value and with unfolding excellence under My leadership. If the mind of the individual is made to embrace a lie or even a portion of a lie about himself or herself, the heart will begin to fail in its function of strength.

A criticism based on an offense … a charge of wrongdoing based on assumption … a judgment based on competition or ego promotion, sends the mind spinning and the heart crashing down in one who has trusted another to be a bearer of truth. At first attack, there is a painful wound inflicted, causing despair to drain the heart of hope. With repeated attacks, the mind in self-protection may try to rebuild its own heart, using rage, accusation, and the power of its own understanding of reality. One broken heart can become encased in self-justification, and then be used to attack the mind, and, therefore, the heart, of another person. Soon, the battle rages. As other people hear of the conflict, their minds may try to find a place of truth and security in the embroiled situation. They, too, join into the conflict, so that a battle between two becomes a battle between several. In the midst of the fray, strongholds form in the mind of the one attacked in order to restore function to a crushed heart. Truth and reality are restructured and altered to raise a wall of defense for the heart. Meanwhile, what now has become the bent reality of the heart?

A crushed heart is fragmented. It has lost a portion of the life blood, which has sustained it in hope and in joy. The heart fibers which were made out of trust, have become frayed and fragile, so that anyone touching the heart can be put under suspicion. Even those coming with My touch to heal the wound can be accused and rejected by the crushed heart under the influence of a deceived mind.

There are times when I choose to lead My sheep through painful paths in order to take them to higher ground. The enemy hides in wait of an opportunity to strike. It is often during this time that those who heed the lies spoken into their minds become a weapon against the hearts of others. Their words sting with accusation increasing the pain upon an already challenged heart. What might have just been a tear in the heart of one can be formed into a pulverizing blow of My enemy though the mouth of another who is deceived. Was it not so with My servant Job as he cried out against the crushing words of those trusted ones, who, led by deception, brought accusation against him? A perverse tongue speaking out of a deceived mind can bring forth great destruction to a heart. Isn't a mouth that speaks charges made out of assumption expressing a form of hatred toward the one whose heart is being crushed by his or her words? I do not look lightly upon such actions. I do not ignore these wounded hearts.

Do not neglect still another truth that I have spoken to you. Often, out of that which is crushed, a snake will arise. Not only is the one speaking deceitfully crushing the heart, but he or she is also making an environment, not for healing and release, but one for deeper bondage to manifest out of the pain inflicted by unholy words.

Be careful little ones! Do not allow your minds to be infused with the lies and misperceptions of the enemy. Do not free your mouths to speak that which emerges from the dark delusions of your own soul … out of the pain of your own unhealed wounds … out of the ferment of unforgiveness for past wrongs done to you that are stored away in your own heart. You have been created to bring forth life and truth. You are to be those who build and restore. If you listen to My enemy's intimations and renditions of truth, acting upon them as if they are reality, you will serve his purposes and counter Mine. It is better to confess being ignorant of truth than to accept as reality a skewed version of it. It is better to be silent than to have your words perverted for evil purposes. It is most wise to come and to consult with Me when you are in conflict, pain or confusion before you utter a sound to another. I long for you to choose healing in order to close the door of access available to My enemy by your unhealed disease. It is My desire that you would receive one source of truth and lay aside your temptation to make sense of your world by creating your own reality, or by agreeing to believe the falsehoods of My enemy.

These are the days of conflict and battle. Be careful not to be blinded while believing yourself to be sighted. In your mind's blindness you may crush the heart of another one in My flock while standing with the enemy of your own soul.

Remember this: I allowed My heart to be crushed by that same enemy, so that in My restoration you could be free to live in truth. I was broken so that you could be healed in your shattered minds and hearts. My life blood was poured out so that you could be partakers of a life beyond your own ability to ever achieve. What does your alliance with falsehood say to

My truth? What do your actions of destruction speak to My actions for your restoration? Do you see the contradiction in the destruction in which you assist when it is held up in the light of My heart? Choose a new course, little ones. Choose a response to the enemy's intimations to your minds that will become a prosperity of the truth, of the life, and of the redemption that My crushed heart has offered to you. You and I working together are to bring restoration to crushed hearts. We together are to be the message of truth. You cannot do these things alone. You cannot do them at all unless you allow Me to be your Source of truth and wholeness.

It is time to arise, for the day of battle is here. The battle is for the minds of my children in order to crush their hearts. Arise to war, using the weapon of My truth. As you arise in Me, you will no longer be inclined to avail yourself to the enemy's use. Instead, you will bring down a crushing blow to the head of this enemy, and, in doing so, you will release the minds and protect the hearts of many.

WHAT IS "PROPHETED"?

———————————————|———————————————

Little ones, it is very important that you are able to hear what I am saying to you. You must not only be able to hear spiritually, you must discern with accurate certainty, verifying that what you are hearing is truly Me. In the days ahead, this ability will become more critical. There is much surrounding noise in the world. Some of it is generated by the clutter and pride of human minds being proclaimed as profound wisdom. Some of the noise is the clashing of kingdoms. Still another source of the perpetual clamor is conflict between human factions presenting opposing versions of reality. Confusion will increase in the world. The urgency to know which way to go will compel the soul to grab hold of whatever sounds like wisdom and truth. This is a dangerous inclination at any time, but it will be deadly in the consuming darkness now coming upon the world. As the darkness encroaches into all areas of human life, the human mind will darken all the more. Human ears will be easily deceived, as urgency replaces cautious consideration, discernment and wisdom. Without discernment, and without the leading of My Spirit, many panicked sheep will follow any voice. Destruction will await them if they follow any leading other than My own.

To assist you in your ability to hear Me accurately, I have sent My Spirit to guide you. I have given the words in My Scriptures to announce to you the truth of My instruction. Teachers, mentors, and leaders have been supplied to show you the way to My Kingdom. Additionally, I have raised up and anointed gifted prophets in every generation to be both My watchmen and My clear voice to the people. During this time, while you sit with Me, consider My servants the prophets.

Even speaking the word "prophet" causes some of My sheep to shudder, while others are given over to great skepticism or opposition. Why is there resistance set up against accepting the fact that I have established these specific servants to be among you? Those of you who have a prophetic call: why do you refuse it? What is profited to My flock when these servants operate faithfully in their anointing and what is lost when they do not? Why are the true prophets so easily ignored and discredited, while the false ones prosper? Consider these things with Me.

First, let Me be very clear. To suggest that there are no longer any of My prophets within the flock is a grave error. It is an arrogance to assume that now, because all in the fold have My Spirit within them, there is no other need for a prophetic presence in human flesh. I have not ceased to raise them up. You have only ceased to recognize and to acknowledge them. In the days to come, the need for these servants will be even greater, as the false prophets of My enemy come into visible power. Without My servants, the prophets, led by My Spirit against these false ones, many in the flock would be deceived.

Certainly, I have created all of My children with equal love and with high value in My eyes. However, it is the human expectation that I have created everyone with equivalent ability and with equal status of authority. This is not true. Distributing a variety of abilities within the flock ensures that the work of My Kingdom is well accomplished. A holy order of command is a reflection of that Kingdom. I have established order and a great variety of gifting within that order. Does My way of singularly endowing certain individuals offend you? Does this mean that I have favorites among the more richly gifted, or that I am arbitrary in the way that I bless and endow? No. I anoint and I bless according to My purposes, not according to your sense of fairness and equality. I bless and establish those in authority according to the heart I see, submitted in obedience, yielding to Me the freedom of personal will. I see these things long before they are observed in the natural by others upon the earth. Often, these precious characteristics escape the view of those who journey in the company of My chosen ones. The world cherishes another set of qualities, while discounting what I cherish most.

Because there is an arrogant resistance against submitting to My authority, there is a natural resistance to the servants I have established to be prophets of My Word among My people. Very often, the truth of My Word has been watered-down, poorly understood, or obscured by those in authority to teach. Rebellion blinds and willfulness deafens the members of My flock and all those who stand in human authority. When a prophet comes along that has been sent by Me, he or she is intended to disquiet the sin within the proud and rebellious. The words of the prophet are sent to open the closed and blinded eyes, as delusions are challenged and as unholy compromises are exposed. I stir the sedentary complacency and the apathetic comfort into uncomfortable motion through the mouths of My prophets. I use these servants to warn and to speak of things yet to come, so that My flock will respond to the words with preparation. At times, I will also call them to speak encouragement, hope, and victory when the flock is in a state of weakness and discouragement. Prophets have a fearful calling … one with a high personal cost. I value them as a vital presence in the flock. You must do the same.

The truth is that the pride of the human heart wants to seek and to maintain its own chosen course. It wants to have its own wisdom validated rather than challenged. Human flesh likes to be exalted, not diminished. Flesh wants the comfort of escape into its excuses, maintained by the convenient ignorance that would be abolished if the flesh were to be brought into close contact with My truth. Furthermore, when a servant who is human comes to challenge other humans, there is the suspicion that the intention of the prophet is to seize power and to control. A corrective or countering voice feels like a threat to individual authority, or a challenge to personal position. Have there been prophets, motivated by anger and offense of their own, wrongfully applying the power of their words? Yes … but fewer than you might think have brought invalid messages. Accountability to Me rests heavily upon the prophets. The heart in which they speak and the validity of their words will be disciplined and dealt with by Me. Even the ones who turned to the seduction of wickedness have been used by Me to deliver the message suiting My purposes. In My flock, there is far greater fear of being deceived or robbed by the power of misguided prophets, than faith in My ability to use them accurately. This must change in the days ahead.

Did you notice I said that the true prophets are Mine, and also Mine to deal with? While that is true, you are not left without the responsibility to discern what is true from what is false. The problem you have with this, quite often, is that you use the wrong measuring tools and scales to make these determinations. If the prophet speaks forcefully you may say that a lack of love disqualifies the speaker. In doing this, you may wrongly ignore the level of love that is pressing the words forth in such strength. Sometimes, words of loving correction can sting and cut. Too often, a forceful, absolute message is discredited, on the basis that surely a messenger of God would not speak in such a way. Where did you get that impression? Has the message of a warm, soft fuzziness surrounding My redemptive love been suggested to you? You forget that both My love and My expression of righteousness are passionate. My zeal, and even My anger, have consumed Me, even after the redemption was accomplished. My character did not change through history, as some surmise. My love was given its ultimate expression in passionate sacrifice, but that passionate love does not negate My intense hatred against wickedness, especially when it is found in My flock. You set a standard of acceptable self-expression for Me that is not congruent with My Word or with My actions demonstrating truth. I am both a tender Shepherd and a consuming fire. Is the fire only applied to My enemies? No. Surely, there is a powerful, refining fire that I send forth upon My own. Be careful not to invalidate a prophet or the word of a prophet because it is strong and disquieting to your peace, to your perspective, or to your position. Ask Me what is truth, and ask without preconceived conclusions in the matter.

Some of you suggest that any word from a prophet that does not bring encouragement or comfort, to build up the flock, is a false message from a false messenger. Again, be careful of your presumption and assumption. Sometimes, building up requires a new, firm foundation to replace a rotten one. The defiled must be struck down as an act of love to prevent loss. Too often, sin in the flock is ignored in favor of bringing messages of encouragement and comfort. Never comfort that which is evil and sinful. It is possible to love the sinner by addressing, in no uncertain terms, the sin that has been embraced, and by announcing where it will lead without a turn in course. Truly, this is the action of one who loves greatly, taking on such a risk of the soul. Gentleness in delivery style, at times, will bring a greater receptivity to the message. Where there is a seriously deceived soul, a quiet, compassionate delivery will often be ignored. My prophets need to be filled with the tone of My Spirit concerning each individual matter, rather than claiming a set format and style … rather than imposing their own climate of soul. Since this is My mandate laid upon the prophet, it would be good for you to agree with it.

If a true message from Me has been spoken or written by a prophet, will it be one hundred per cent accurate? By its very definition it must be. I speak only truth. If I speak through a prophet of Mine, it must be completely true. The application or translation of the word by the prophet or by the recipient may be in error, causing the word itself to seem false. The timing of its fulfillment may be for a distant time in the future, giving the impression of an erroneous message and messenger. Again, be careful. Do not trust a prophet who accepts anything less than one hundred per cent accuracy, but do not determine the accuracy or inaccuracy on your own. Likewise, do not seek after the meaning of the message nor its application by using the power of your own soul, or the counsel of the flesh. Seek Me. Compare the utterance to My Word. It will not disagree with what I have already spoken. Again, be careful that you see and read with divinely inspired eyes … hearing with divinely inspired ears and with a pure heart, or again you will be misled to discredit what is real. Conversely, if you neglect to use divine opinion and instead use your own or popular opinion to determine the validity, meaning, or application, you will again fall into error. Know this: My prophets can and must present My messages to the flock with perfect accuracy. To allow for a little error to be acceptable as the word comes through a human mouth is to open a dangerous door. There is no such thing as practicing to speak prophetically until you learn to speak in accuracy. The practice comes first in listening and learning to know My voice, and then in practicing obedience, delivering what I have said.

Consider these things I have told you. Become familiar with what is a true prophet and a true word, before you explore the realities of counterfeit prophets and of false words. If you effectively learn to recognize what is true and what is of Me, it will be easy to discern what is bogus. Too often, My little ones invest much of their focus upon what is not of My Kingdom … in this case focusing on false prophets … before they learn what is truly of Me. This inverted priority and negative process of learning leads many astray. They emerge from their study of the false with a hyper suspicion of all that is good and Godly. Invest in the true first, so that you will be drawn to it rather than to the false.

The false prophets will be identified clearly in the Spirit. Take note of some common traits that they will demonstrate. The false prophets will seek after the influence and power of the wealthy. They will establish the direction of their messages in accordance to the most benefit available to them. Emotionally, they will be unstable with no steady foundation of peace. They will seek honor and homage for themselves, taking as much glory as the lost will give them. They will have cold hearts which are easily offended, but never offering forgiveness. Self-justification, power, and control will be their priority. They will have flattering tongues except when it comes to condemning My little ones. They will be found in governmental positions, in seats of justice, and in churches. They will have a form of religion, professing godliness, but they will be

147

devoid of My character and apart from My presence. They will seduce you and threaten you to gain your submission. To submit is to be subverted. You must know My voice. You must know My Word. You must know My true prophets.

Finally, I want you to know what is at stake in the days ahead if you neglect the true prophetic. My true prophets will battle and call down the false ones. My true prophets will give insight and wisdom from My Kingdom in a time when confusion reigns and a famine of truth covers the earth. My true prophets will bring forth visionary dreams and interpretations of dreams, giving valuable keys to My people in the midst of spiritual war. Signs and wonders will be commanded through them, encouraging the flock and astounding those who seek truth from outside of the flock. My true prophets will labor in intercession and cry out until they receive the help and instruction My flock desperately needs. When error is being spoken from every corner of the earth, My prophets will break through the lies to announce My truth. They will serve notice to wicked leaders and they will prophesy to the harvest, bringing it forth. Gates will open and walls will come down as My servants speak. Many of these servants will be killed at the hands of false prophets, but they will not cease to labor on behalf of My Kingdom. Because of their steadfast testimony, many members of My flock will be encouraged to take their stand. Do you now understand what you will lack if you do not allow My prophets to come into their ordained positions in your midst? I do not set them up to be admired by you, or so that you will listen to them instead of Me for yourselves. Instead, I call you to know My voice so that the leading of My Spirit within you will be confirmed by them.

Trust My plan to provide for you. The functioning of the prophets in the final hours of the earth is part of that plan and provision. Humble yourselves, prophets! Humble yourselves, all those in the company of the prophets. Work together to accomplish My purposes. This is to be your finest hour, little ones. My Kingdom will profit from your work. Victory and strength will be yours. Fulfill your calling, and allow all My servants to fulfill theirs … including the prophets.

UNITY AND MUTINY

Little ones, do you laugh at the thought of a flock of sheep being an army? How silly that seems when you consider the nature of sheep. They spend their days munching grass, strolling about, or napping under a tree. When the shepherd calls for the flock to arise and move to new pastures, they respond and follow, knowing that fresh food and vital water will meet them in that place. When the shepherd leads the sheep to a safe enclosure to spend the night, they are wise to follow the shepherd's lead, submitting to his wisdom for shelter. In the same way, you are to be obedient and expectant to My call. But you, My precious ones, you are to be a peculiar sort of sheep. In your sacrificial obedience to Me, you become much more than a grass-masticating wanderer.

I have ordained each one in My flock to follow after Me— in the heart and in the gentle tenderness of a lamb. However, I have also created each of you to have teeth when it comes to taking a stand against an advancing enemy. For the purposes of victory in war, I am your authority in all things. However, even as an army has levels of earned or assigned leadership under the highest authority, I too have assigned authorities of leadership over you. My requirement for you is to follow My lead explicitly. To do this faithfully, it is necessary for you to understand that those I have assigned to lead you and to teach you, imparting My instruction to you, are also given for your submission. Consider this truth with Me.

I have called you to be in total submission to My leadership, following Me wherever I lead, but I have wanted more from you than convenient, self-sustaining obedience. My heart is to position you for victory in every battle. Every victory is enabled by the sacrificial obedience that arises only from a surrendered heart of deep love and devotion. Surely, I have the power to control you, but, because of My covenant at the beginning of time, I have set you free to choose Me or to choose your own way. That makes Me a unique Shepherd and gives you the possibility of being an extraordinary sheep.

It is written and declared that the God of Israel is echad … ONE. This is a certain truth, but one that is often hard to grasp. This divine echad is an expression of unity in integral, distinct facets, not just a singularity as humans understand it. I am the ultimate echad. Even so, I call My sheep to also become a form of echad with each other as I enable them to move as distinctive individuals and yet as one flock. It is not possible for unity of function to be maintained if unity of priority is broken by division. Have you not seen the brokenness that comes from self-promotion or rebellion out of self-interest? Even as there must be one Shepherd and one flock, so, also, there must be one heart priority, with all members of the flock positively submitting to that unity, established and expressed by My heart for them.

Consider the term, "positively submitting." Why would I use that expression? Obedience can be offered freely or it can be demanded and enforced. When it is freely given to Me, the fruit of that obedience becomes life-giving and life-sustaining. If, however, the obedience is nothing more than an acquiescence to someone more powerful demanding it from you, a door is left open in the heart to rebellion and to mutiny. Over time, the negativity of the soul will seek to break out to express its resentment from being under authority. Positive submission is a gift of trust and a sacrifice of one's own power so that the one in assigned authority can move the flock forward in wisdom and strength.

Consider this application when leadership is placed above you in human form. For one who has been suspicious of empowered human authority, jealous to possess it for oneself, or still living out of the sting of feeling powerless somewhere in personal history, positive submission is very difficult. Such a member of the flock can move successfully in cooperation with the leader assigned by Me, but only for a limited time. At first, the blessing of such leadership can be seen and experienced, but, over time, the benefits become harder to embrace. Initially, submission may come with a heart desiring personal growth and group unity, but an open door in the heart allows those desires to drain away over time. Pain and jealousy provide listening ears for the words of self-promotion, for fears of being suppressed, and for illusions of being less valued than the one placed in authority over a portion of My flock. Out of this ferment of the soul, mutiny begins to form unseen. The desire to glean from the leadership fades. The heart, once seeking the power of unity, begins to take on the priority of personal power and validation. Submission to My assigned leadership changes allegiance, even though, for a while, there will be a feigned impression of being submitted. There may even be calculated steps taken to endear the one of simmering rebellion to the heart of the leader in order to come closer to the power of leadership.

Consider another manifestation which gives the appearance of submission, but which is looking for a way to break out. Contempt ... contempt for personal insufficiency seen in the light of someone else's abilities ... will often arise as comparison and competition begin speaking entitlement into the soul of the one being called to submit. The thoughts of contempt gather over time. They appear at first as mere questions inspired by My enemy pressing on the soul of one of My sheep. In reality, they are the inclinations of the Accuser. "What qualifies him or her to lead over you?" "Do you not see the control, the sin, and the pride being demonstrated?" "Are you not equally gifted or sufficiently skilled to lead as this one taking charge over you?" After the questions will come the conclusions, spoken as self-talk into the questioning soul: "Surely this is an unqualified/self-promoted leader." "If I give up my power in submission to this one, I will be seen having less honor and value in the eyes of those around me." "Surely this leader will lead me to weakness or to my destruction. I must not place myself under such controlling authority." "Surely the Shepherd wants me to stand apart in order to draw more deeply from Him personally." "For the sake of the other sheep, I must rise up and speak for their release."

If these questions, inspired by fallen flesh or by My enemy, are not rejected ... if the conclusions are accepted and if they take root ... it is only a small matter of time until rebellion is formed. Mutiny ... which is to inspire others to share and to support you in the rebellion ... is close at hand. If power and authority cannot be seized through the power of words to convince the leader to stand aside, My enemy will inspire the jealous/deceived one to establish his or her own place of authority, taking a number of the other sheep to walk under his or her leadership. Often in an effort to justify the mutiny, those of unsubmitted hearts discredit the leadership by striking him or her down by falsehoods, gossip, and assumptions.

How shall I respond to mutiny against one whom I have put into leadership under My authority? If I have established, shall I not also have the right to remove? Is the problem that you do not understand it is I Who have placed leadership into positions of power for My purposes? You so fear that the self-promotion operative in your own heart is the motivation of the heart of the other. You assume that the one in leadership has placed himself or herself in that position. You err, little ones, when you think that anyone is in position without My design at work. I position people in leadership for the good of the flock. I know what that flock requires for health and for training. What is it to you if I call you to submit to leadership that breaks your flesh, or which calls you more deeply into dependency upon Me? What if I choose to bring to you a leader which will expose your own darkness of heart and press upon the wounds you have hidden? What if I choose to bring to you leaders who challenge your understanding and who drive you into the truth of My Word? Do you see that discomfort as a blessing to you? Truly, it is My blessing placed upon your journey. I have intentionally chosen to give you leaders that are imperfect, even as I have chosen them to be human. Are you offended by their imperfections? Do you demand things of them that can only be demanded of Me ... things which you are not able to accomplish? Consider your heart quickly. Weigh your actions and your words. Any mutiny against what I have established for the flock will have severe consequences.

Those who claim to submit to My leadership but who initiate mutiny against what I have established, will be taken to a place of humiliation by Me. Those who rise up to claim gifting and position that are not given to them by Me, will lose even the precious things I have entrusted to them for their fulfillment and for their joy. Why do I respond so severely in this matter of mutiny? I respond in this way because mutiny was the way that the dominion of darkness was born. It is the hallmark of that dark dominion. The unity of heaven was broken by the mutiny of one who sought to seize and to claim what was not his nor ever could be. Had these inclinations in the heart of one been repented of, I would have been merciful. However, without repentance and with a profound, blinding pride, the mutiny against Me was raised. Every day of your lives, you feel the price of that rebellion. Should I not also deal severely with such inclinations in the members of My flock? This is not just a matter of challenge against My leadership when such things occur in the flock, it is a way for My flock to be defeated in battle and destroyed. For Me to respond severely in such matters is a sign of My great love and of My great desire for you to be victorious in every battle.

Have you not seen the fruit of rebellion in the physical body? Cancer is a manifestation of cell division in rebellion to My order. It is a sign of another authority seeking to assert itself and to build structures that have not been ordained by Me, following a design not of Me. The outcome is pain, dysfunction, and sometimes even death. Am I saying that all those little ones who are stricken with cancer are ones of rebellion to My leadership and order? No. What cancer presents is a parable of the cost of rebellion so that the hearts of those in My flock can understand the cost of mutiny as it supplants unity and moves apart from divine order. The message is clear. Rebellion against what I have established can be deadly. It can weaken the flock unless it is excised and radically treated. Not even a single cell of it can be allowed to remain. Those who rise up against Me and against the leadership I have established over them put themselves at risk of being the virus used by My enemy to bring weakness, death, and defeat into the flock. I cannot bless stolen authority. I cannot defend those in mutiny. My blessing comes to those in submission to Me, to My Word, to My way, and to My authority.

Unity in the flock is My heart for you. I have created the opportunities, bestowed the gifting, and ordered the steps of My flock to bring forth victory. Each member has been entrusted with a role to play. Each one has a weapon to use. No one in My flock is without power. Perhaps the greatest power I have given you is the power to choose. You must positively choose to follow My lead and the lead of those I have placed in your life to guide you. You must not agree to the course outwardly while inwardly fostering thoughts of rebellion and resentment. To do so makes you an easy target to bring destruction into the work of My flock, and loss into your own life. Unity is not uniformity … it does not make you without distinction in the flock. Each of you is unique and uniquely positioned and anointed. No one is insignificant. Your need to find a place for yourself, rather than appreciating the place in which I have assigned you, will make you vulnerable to the deceptions of the enemy, leading you to pride and then into mutiny.

The enemy dreads the flock standing and moving in unity under divine leadership. Such unity is the source of certain and swift defeat for him. Do you understand now why this is such a recurring problem in the flock? Do you see your own vulnerability in this matter? No army can be victorious in battle unless it is fully and obediently submitted to the established order of command and authority. No army can be successful unless the demands of training are satisfied by rigorous submission to the program required for the soldiers. Those who will not submit in boot camp to the sergeant calling them to discipline, and to painful training maneuvers, will not be promoted to positions of higher authority. Opportunities for using their potential power will be denied the rebellious recruit. Officers of higher rank will not be promoted to greater commands over the troops unless they accomplish well what is required of them in their current position, and unless they submit fully to the highest authority of leadership. They may not fully understand the strategies. They may not fully appreciate the required discipline. Understanding the ways and the reasons are not preconditions for giving submission to authority. The only precondition is to know WHO is in command and WHO has the authority to lead. In time, understanding of the ways and reasons for the orders will come.

Little ones, do you fear being led or abused by wrongful authority more than you trust My ability and faithfulness to set proper authority over you? Lay aside this fear. Do you despise your own sense of insufficiency more than you embrace My all-encompassing sufficiency? Trust Me to provide those around you to lead you as I lead them. Have you been tempted into rebellion by your jealous heart? Refuse the inclinations to compare yourself to others or to pick up a spirit of competition against them. If you truly understand who you are in Me, these things will be of little concern to you. As you come into the knowledge of My delight, in My design of you, you will become aware that My chosen way for you will only lead you to fulfillment … not to frustration.

Arise, flock … come into unity so that you may come into victory. Hear the call to accept the rigors of the training I have set for you. Hear My voice in the leaders calling you to submission. If there is ever a voice that is not Mine speaking over you … if there is ever a wrong order given … I shall personally deal with it. Remember that the chief general disciplines those of rank under his leadership. Do not open the doorway to rebellion and to mutiny by taking matters into your own hands. Do not run away to establish your own training and your own authority. Your evaluation of the situation will always be lacking. The enemy will seize opportunities in the midst of your lack, if you move away from My order. When you believe that you are being wrongly led, come to Me with your concerns. Ask Me to show you how to submit and how to keep you heart pure while I sort out the situation. Discover what I intend for you to learn. Remember, any places of wounding or darkness in your heart will enable you to hear deception and to believe it as truth. Come to Me for healing now. Repent of your pride and lay aside your fears established out of past history. Positively submit to My sovereignty and you will absolutely achieve victory.

Know that I always consider the heart in all My children. Each heart has depths which you cannot see. These unseen depths are in both your heart and in the heart of the one you may be tempted to accuse. Matters of interpreting, judging, and exposing the depths of any heart are best left with Me. Make your priority the desire to stand with Me, serving My purposes, even when you lack understanding of what is happening within you and around you. When each of you stand with Me in My purposes, and when each of you move together, marching in your assigned authority, we form an invincible reality. The flock and the Shepherd experience absolute unity. When the battle is won, we will delight together in eternal joy.

WHAT ARE YOU FIGHTING FOR?

Where is your true home and homeland, little ones? Soldiers fight for their homeland and for those who belong to that territory. They fight because of a heart of passion to preserve their precious home territory from invasion and takeover. They fight to declare their allegiance and to protect their inheritance. True, there are those, who are mercenaries ... paid soldiers available for hire to support any cause. My warriors will NEVER be mercenaries, even though many of the warriors who fight against My Kingdom truly sell themselves for a price.

The present mindset of world is formulated by those who do not acknowledge or honor Me. These supposed "enlightened ones," are living under the illusion that they possess the status of human divinity. They wield their own prescribed power and authority based upon human, intellectually-determined correctness. These deceived ones declare that any form of war is repulsive and immoral. In that My Word clearly speaks of the necessity of conducting physical and spiritual war at times, they utterly reject Me as an authority and as a reality. They charge that there is no such thing as absolute evil or absolute good. They arrogantly defend this delusion in spite of My Word declaring the opposite, and in spite of an abundance of evidence confirming that they are operating in blind error. They have no homeland, because, in their reckoning, those who claim national identities are seen as divisive and wrongfully territorial. They see national identities, and human moral unfairness, along with the unequal distribution of resources among the world's populations, as being the problematic origins of war. Their worldview champions a global unity, where all human aspirations are the same, valid, and good. They see that all human concepts have a valid right to manifest, except for any belief, standard, or declaration that suggests their humanist concepts are wrong.

Their goal is to eliminate war and conflict, by creating a one world family that abides by a uniform, humanly-created code, and by eventually operating under the order of a single global ruler. According to their assessments, nationalities, boundaries, and borders cause conflict; therefore, these things must be eliminated globally. Boldly, they champion this worldview as the only true reality ... this in spite of the fact that I intentionally divided up the human creation into specific tribes and nations. I created the varying tongues and languages, and I declared these things to be good. It is My will for each person to belong to a family or a tribe ... to a nation ... and to My Kingdom. Why would this awareness and acknowledgement be important in the day of battle? If you don't know your true home, you will refuse to fight, or you will stand with any power that gives your flesh the benefits it seeks. If you see spiritual war as unacceptable, unnecessary, or fictitious, you will distain the warriors who arise in battle to defend their homeland.

This delusion leaves precious territory undefended at best, and surrendered at worst. It brings forth an unholy tolerance of evil and manifests in costly, erroneous, judgements. This is exactly what the enemy is counting on to give him an advantage in the fight.

So what will you fight for, little ones? What do you see as your home, and your homeland? You need to claim these things in the physical domain and, also, in the spiritual jurisdiction. First, consider your physical, earthly home and homeland. Do you see these things as gifts from Me? Do you see your place of residence and your nationality as an endowment for your family line, and as a launching pad for your earthly destiny? Truly, they are appointed to you by My authority. Your vision of My plan to bless you, is so limited that perhaps you do not see your tribal and national assignment as a blessing. Perhaps you are very discontented with where I have planted you. You will not be willing to fight and to defend that which you are unwilling to value. Are you willing to trust Me in My placement for you? Are you willing to look, with fresh eyes, at the place where you now dwell? If My hand chooses to move you to a new, physical location, that will not change your human lineage genetic. You will remain in possession of the same DNA that connects you to your family line, to your gender, and to your tribal distinctions, which I fashioned when you were created. Citizenship may change with residency, but My chosen root for you does not change. It is to be a blessing to you, but not a prideful obsession. Those who flaunt their human genetics, as if it is superior to others, commit a great offense against Me and against all of the human creation. Only I have the authority to assign, and to declare, special significance or status to any nation, tribe, or family line.

Always be mindful that your position and your genetics are never to become an idolatry. You are never to serve or to cherish your physical home, family, and homeland above Me. Celebrate where you are and who you are, always seeking to discover how your life can best serve Me. Be willing, and be prepared to defend your physical home and homeland, and the lives therein, whenever I call you forth … even if that means you will go into physical battle. Do not initiate soulish conflict, nor enter into battle without My call to arms. If you do advance without Me, and if you battle soul against soul, much unnecessary destruction will occur.

Now, consider your spiritual home and homeland. Some of you little ones would report that your spiritual home is your congregation or denomination. That would be an error. In reality, your only spiritual home must be IN ME. In this reality, you will always BE HOME. I am to be your abiding place. I am to be your place of rest and protection. I am to be the place where you grow in truth and in knowledge of the truth. Remember that I created you to be part of a living, spiritual body, where each member contributes his or her gifting and service to the magnificent creation that operates under My headship. You were not intended to find your identity in a group or in a building, but only in ME. As for your spiritual homeland, that is the place where you will abide throughout all eternity with Me. My High Kingdom is your homeland. This world is merely a proving ground and a great adventure for those who truly embrace Me. One day, I will call you back to your homeland. It will be familiar to you upon arrival. Before you came to earth, your spirit knew Me there. Those who fear death do not understand that earth is not their homeland. You are merely a sojourner here for a time. It is ordained that you would both return home to Me in this life and, also, return to dwell in your eternal homeland, when your earthly life is finished. Until that time, when your life in this world ends, I want you to cherish the homeland that I have established for you here on the earth. Care for it and defend it as a trust for, and from, Me.

Now that the questions of home and homeland have been clarified in both the physical and spiritual realms, the questions become: Are you willing to fight for what I declare is a righteous cause upon the earth? Are you willing to contend for the faith against the threats of false religions and against rebellious philosophies and rules? Are you willing to take a stand against perversions that contradict My way, will, and Word? Are you willing to lay down your life to declare and to defend My Kingdom? Will you defend life, order, and law as I have commanded these things? You will only fight for what you value and love. Do you value Me and love Me, above all else? Some will say that there is no need to stand in My defense … that I can defend Myself very well. Those, who say such things, are leaving a door open for themselves, so that they can escape the battle. I am constantly watching and listening to see if My children love and value Me and My Kingdom enough to take a stand for it … to fight for it when needed. Sadly, some prefer to deny and to avoid the responsibilities that come from being a member in My family. They will find out in the final accounting that I don't recognize them as part of My Kingdom, because they took the blessings but refused to participate in the Kingdom when it was personally too costly, too unpopular, or too inconvenient. These self-possessed ones refused to give Me their lives, but, instead, chose to keep charge of their own destiny, and to create their own course of life, while simply going through the motions of being a member of My household. They will never experience how gloriously transformed they could have been by living in Me and for Me— beyond themselves. They will never know the unending joy and glory of being with Me for eternity.

Tragically, many of My little ones have bought into the lie

that all conflict is bad, and that appeasement and acquiesce are good. Before sin entered into lucifer, and before sin entered into the hearts of My human creations, there was no conflict. Indeed, all was good. However, once sin appeared, a perpetual conflict formed between My Kingdom and the Kingdom of darkness. The manifestations of this ongoing war have been readily visible throughout the history of the world. In this season of the earth, the conflict is increasing to a degree that has never before been seen. It is impossible to avoid the conflict. If you align your life with My Kingdom, you will automatically be at war with the Kingdom of darkness. Those who align themselves with the darkness will automatically be in direct conflict with Me, and with those who align with My Kingdom. If anyone in My human creation tries to live half way between these two Kingdoms at war … in order to avoid having to take sides … being uncommitted to both … I will account that person as having rejected Me in favor of My enemy. You are either fully FOR Me, or completely against Me. There is no doorway into the heavenly homeland found in the middle ground. To think otherwise is pure foolishness, and the fruit of deep deception.

Little ones, you must know this! NEVER make peace with a lie, and never allow the enemies of My Kingdom to have access to your appointed territory. When conflict rises up to meet you, seek Me quickly for your response and strategy. Take a stand. Shout a warning. Fire a shot of holy decree into the air. As I lead, pick up your weapons and fight. If cancer ever invaded your body, threatening it with death, wouldn't you fight passionately to drive out that deadly invader? Why, then, do you allow false doctrines, and rebellious standards of morality, and many other things which bear the stench of hell on them, to move into your territory or into your family, without taking up a battle stance against them? I have been watching the enemy encroach upon your strategic territory and upon your precious inheritance. Too often, I see apathy or abandonment regarding My standards, and compliance to the demands of the evil one. This must never be your position. You are to be decisive, discerning, and wise in the ways of war. You are to be aware of the enemy's tactics and advances. You are to cut him off with every advance.

Pick up your weapons for the battle, little ones, but only pick up the weapons that I have provided. Put on your whole set of armor that I have offered to you. Pick up the chief weapons of holiness: humility, submission, obedience, and love. Do not modify these weapons to accommodate the popular world-view. Operate in holy obedience and in submission to My way, will, and Word. Do not redefine My definition of love, nor re-format My rules. Be willing to defend truth, and to fight for it. However, make sure that the truth you defend is really MY TRUTH, and not a soulish, human version of it.

It's time that you, My little ones, lay aside all pettiness, and cease all foolish skirmishes, which are based upon opinions, pride, and jealousy. Do you not see that the enemy has intentionally sent contention and division into your midst so that you will fight each other, rather than attacking his schemes? Wake up and become wise, little ones! Discern what is real, and what is contrived delusion. Subdue your flesh. See, hear, think, and respond out of the Spirit, not out of your soul. See the true enemy and become wise to his tricks. Take note of those who are his human operatives and develop spiritual discernment to know who they are who walk the earth in allegiance to him. Discern the presence and the activities of the evil one's invisible servant and allies. At the same time, come to recognize those who are My true disciples and warriors. Discern those who claim Me in name only, while building their own kingdoms. Trust only those who have found their identity in

Me and those who will lay down their lives for My Kingdom … for their home and homeland.

The day of battle is at hand. I am crying out to you. Come forth! Consider who you are! Know where you stand … then take that stand and hold it. If you fight for your own cause, your battle will be futile. If you fight with man-made weapons, you will fail in spiritual war. If you hesitate to engage the enemy once I have sent forth the battle cry, you could be quickly overrun. Your territory could be seized. It is My will that you be glorious in victory for Me and for My Kingdom. I will enable you to stand and to conquer. Decide now what you are willing to fight for, even to the cost of your own earthly life. Settle right now the issue of surrender. Set your hearts on total surrender to Me, so that you will never surrender anything to the enemy. Then, watch Me lead you into the battle. I will guarantee Kingdom victory, even when it appears to be defeat. For those who fight for Me, using My weapons and following My leading, there is never an occasion of defeat. When it appears that the enemy is winning, watch and pray. I will allow the enemy to advance for a season, so that his confidence and pride will rise. Then, suddenly, I will engage My warriors with a crushing blow, delivering him and his armies a humiliating defeat.

Arise in the truth. Arise in your commitment to defend My truth. Arise and face the enemy. As you fight for your true home and homeland, I will deliver the enemy into your hands. This I promise: I will always fight at your side, assuring you the victory until I return you to the homeland where you will eternally abide with Me. KNOW what you are fighting for, and then arise and fight when you hear My cry!

OUT OF THE FIRE

Do you hear the war machine of the enemy, little ones? The fires of hell are stoking a great furnace of hatred, division, perversion, and rebellion among my human creations. Demon horsemen have mounted the minds and hearts of many of My children and are already riding on the souls of multitudes. The forges within the dark kingdom are burning hot. Every available source of human metal is being smelted into weapons to be used against Me and against My faithful ones. A great, wicked, war machine is forming for a great battle. The temperature of the spiritual climate is becoming hotter each day.

Weapons comprised of hateful, deceitful, violent words are being launched into the public arenas, and, yet, these attacks are only the beginning salvos of what is yet to come. These destructive fire bombs, that are launched from the lips of my human creations, cause a shout of great delight to arise in the dark realm. "More recruits for us," they shout! "More humiliation for the Holy One, as His ways are refused by men!" For a time, it will appear that the forces of darkness and hatred are winning the battle. Surely, they have garnered more members for their army than is readily seen in Mine. But do not fear, little ones. I have divine forces that greatly outnumber the forces of evil. I have plans for the days ahead. I have hidden away glorious plans that will be enacted by My faithful ones. It's time that you prepare. Even now, I have sent forth a cry for My armies to assemble and for My faithful ones to come into a deeper intimacy with Me ... and into a deeper unity with each other. Heed My cry, and come into My presence to prepare for what is to come.

As you begin to mobilize for spiritual battle, know that I will never leave you, betray you, nor set you up for destruction. It's important that you understand this and believe it. Surely, there will be losses and pain in the midst of battle, but I am not putting you in the front lines, so that I can hide behind you. I will be completely attentive to your heart and to your needs. I will always stand in front of you as your shield, even as I will be a surrounding presence and a wall of protection behind you. You will not suffer anything that I will not be suffering with you, but I will always suffer to a greater degree. When you cry out in pain or in loss, the enemy will be quick to accuse My love for you as being false, little ones. Do not believe his lies. His desire is that you would curse Me for abandoning you, so that the power that comes from holy sacrifices offered up in love, will not materialize. Trust me, little ones. There are mysteries of spiritual battle that you do not understand. Know this: I will open your eyes to see the victory in midst of apparent loss. I will open your eyes to behold the glory that will dawn upon you with every sacrifice offered up in love. Listen for My voice and trust in My love. Allow Me to lead you through the fire to what lies beyond.

There are times when sacrifices need to be made to increase the authority and power of My human troops. When holy blood is shed, redemption comes ... victory breaks forth. Any loss that you experience will be an assured advancement against the enemy, as you follow My commands. It may be difficult for you to understand, but a life completely surrendered to Me, in complete love and trust, always sweeps the feet of the enemy. The evil one can only goad his followers onward by his mocking, by his threats, and by making deceitful promises of a higher status and power for those who serve him. He rages each time that he sees My little ones, choosing to serve Me by laying down their lives out of love for Me. When the frightening fire appears before you, take My hand and allow Me to walk you through that fire.

There will be times when the fire will be a thin veil of threat. Once you courageously pass through it, you will expose and defeat whatever you find operating behind it. There will be times when the fire will be at your feet. In those moments, go quickly to worship and to praise, declaring who I AM. Before you realize it, you will find yourself rising above the fire, and walking over the top of it, unharmed. There will be times when the fire will be over your head. Move into a position of lowly humility before Me. Ask Me to quench the fire, and I will be quick to cut off the breath that empowers it. There will be times when the fire comes in blazing spears, seeking to pierce your chest to stop your heart. Apply your shield of faith, and believe that I hold your destiny in My hand and that I alone decree your worth and identity in truth.

In the days ahead, the enemy will bring forth the fires of attrition. He will try to deplete you in every way, by depleting the supply of material substance and by cutting you off from those who would give you support. He will try to convince you that you are all alone. He will arrogantly offer you a way to survive by yielding to his leadership, rejecting Mine. Never consider his offer. Full well, He knows that I am standing right there with you. But he also knows that you need to acknowledge Me to experience the manifestation of the truth of My presence ever with you. Allowing satan to threaten you is a test that I may decide to entrust to you. Declaring me in the face of satanic fire humiliates him and drives him backward. Each victory in Me will give you greater power and authority over the darkness. Every loss, when met by the 7-fold restitution which My Word promises is yours, will become a mighty gain for both you, and for My Kingdom.

Now, I want to speak to you about the matter of fireproofing My little ones. Think back upon the massive challenge My three servants faced generations ago in the midst of Babylon. Having been brought before the king on charges of rebellion against a regal decree, Shadrach, Meshach and Abednego stood firm. Without compromising and without apology, these three warriors took a stand in the face of mortal fire. Nebuchadnezzar had arrogantly declared himself to be god and had demanded that every human being fall in worship before his own image cast in gold. My servants respectfully refused and told the king that the issue was settled in their hearts. Under no conditions would they give their worship to anyone other than to Me. No other god would be declared as their Sovereign Lord. The king was confident that the threat of the fiery furnace would change their minds, but his pride was humiliated by their statements of reply. They declared that I was capable of saving them, but, if I chose not to, I was no less God, and they would worship no other. You may remember that the furnace was made to become seven times hotter. As a result, the soldiers, who tossed them into the furnace were immediately consumed in the blaze, but My intact servants met ME in the fire. Together, we walked about in the comfort of shalom, which comes from being fire-proofed through intimate faith. These faithful three willingly laid their lives on My altar and trusted Me to do what would bring forth a Kingdom victory. Their confident faith, expressed in spoken decree, fireproofed them. I could have chosen to lift their spirits out of burning bodies, promoting them into the glorious rewards of My High Kingdom's dwelling. That would have been a blessing to them. However, a greater, Kingdom gain was in My plan. Bringing a deluded monarch to the moment of declaring My reality as Sovereign Lord ... positioning him so that he would broadcast the reality of My glory and power, which was demonstrated through My three servants ... actually melted the gate into Hades that the evil one had set up in Nebuchadnezzar's kingdom. That tremendous advancement against evil would not have been possible unless My fireproofed servants had been willing to go into the fire, so that I might lead them out in victory. It must be the same for you, little ones.

A day is coming upon the earth, very soon, when evil will be so completely invasive into the very fabric of government, education, media, commerce, and throughout all of society, that wicked voices in power will demand obedience or death. Such levels of threat and control will be horrifically intimidating to the masses. They will bow ... they will comply ... they will do whatever is demanded in order to stay alive. And this will be the great test of My chosen ones. I have already given you the examples of Daniel, of Shadrach, Meshach, and Abednego, of Paul, and of countless others, who have already been victorious in the overwhelming test. The anointings of great courage, of steadfast faith, and of solid confidence that they demonstrated in the face of death will also be there for you in your time of testing. Now is the time to exercise your faith. Now is the time to take courageous steps against the smaller threats.

Now is the time for practicing confidence in Me, by taking the steps that I have ordained for you to take against the grain of evil decrees and practices. If you lack faith, little ones, ask Me for a great endowment of faith. However, once you have been given that gift, you must apply it for it to become embedded … even programmed into your thinking and responding as you face challenges. Faith, when exercised, becomes stronger. Courage, when applied to little threats, will grow to become victorious over great threats. When you ask Me to give you confidence, I will say to you, "Come in closer to know Me more intimately." In this way, your confidence will spontaneously blossom and grow. As you know more of Me, you will realize how deeply I love you, and how deeply I care for your heart. Your welfare is greatly regarded by Me, but even more is My attention given to the fulfillment of your victorious destiny.

Do not fear the friendly fire that I will bring into your life to refine you into pure gold. The chaff will be burned away, and your heart will be cleansed to a deeper level of purity. Pride will be burned into sweet humility. Doubt will be consumed and replaced by faith. Timidity will be refined into courage. Your need of Me in the fire of adversity, is intended to formulate an invitation for Me to come in closer for a more intimate embrace with you. As you cry out, I come and encompass you, in order to lift you higher.

Yes, the enemy will bring his fire of war against you. Do not fear him, for he is already defeated … full well, he knows it. What he is counting on is that My little ones will not know that truth. He wants them to fear him and to cower under his threats and perverse power. But, I want you to not only know the truth, but to walk into the fire declaring it. We WILL do this together. I WANT to do this with you. Know that I will be with you in the midst of the fire, and, together, we shall walk out of the fire into victorious glory. We will go into the fire together, and we will emerge together, dancing in the delight of the enemy's defeat.

This I promise you. Just believe. I am with you ALWAYS … EVERYWHERE.

COMMITMENT AND GLORY

Little ones, let My Word fill your mouth. Let My glory fill your mind, that you may know Me anew. Empty your mind of all human understanding and listen to My Word.

The season of the Refiner's fire is here, out of which will emerge a holy nation, and a royal priesthood of My precious ones. At last, the longing of My heart shall be satisfied. You have been seeking Me to receive knowledge of the role you are to play in this time, as well as the position you are to fill. It is a delight to Me that you come to inquire concerning these things. Truly I say, you will enter the fire to be refined and purified during these days. It is a gift that I give to those, who seek My face as well as My hand. It is My desire that My lambs shine with the glory of My presence in these days. It is My longing that what flows from their lips is filled with the power of truth and love. I yearn for you to walk in the authority that comes from integrity. Therefore, what has been professed by the lips, and felt in the heart, must become the consuming power of your spirit. There must be both a consistency and an integrity that is birthed through intimacy with Me. I have carried you upon My shoulders, little ones, when you were too weak to walk on your own. I have held you to My breast and allowed you to hear the beating of My heart. My voice has become familiar to you, and you have learned from both watching Me and listening to My instruction. Now, you will enter into a new level of commitment. There will be no discrepancies between profession of the heart, the mouth, and activity of the hands and feet. There will be complete agreement. These are the days of proceeding glory and total commitment.

Have you ever watched a mountain climber ascending a sheer mountain face? Where will he find a place to rest his foot or a place to affix in his grasp? His journey upward must be accomplished with great patience and with great commitment to his goal. He must take with him all that is necessary for a successful climb and only that which is needed. His hands must be available to use what is essential to create the way to become successful. With great effort, he will drive the nails into the cracks of the mountain, making a place for his foot and for his harness. He must choose wisely and carefully, for his very life depends upon his choice. There must be a determined inner voice calling him upward when his body tires from the rigors of the climb. As night falls, he must be prepared to stop where there is no stopping place. With a sure hand and a trusting heart, he pounds in the nail that will support the weight of his body as it rests in a sling high above the ground. Is this not an act of total commitment? To entrust your life into the keeping of a totally supporting structure in a dangerous situation is an act of great faith and of great courage. As he continues, in wisdom, holding fast to his commitment of the climb … he will arrive at the time of glory … standing upon the heights of the mountain peak … beholding the wonders known only to the successful climber.

Little ones, this parable applies to all who would journey upward in the spirit during these days of great challenge. Those who wish to climb to the heights of authority, vision, and glory, known only in My Kingdom, will do so only as they proceed in total commitment. This is not the journey for the self-protected or for those who are double-minded. Many will long for the glory of the arrival at the mountain peak, only to turn away in fear that fills the heart when standing at the foot of the sheer mountain face. This is not the journey for those who climb to be admired and honored for their achievements, for they will not have enough life and death commitment to climb more than a small distance before returning to the base. No, this climb will be reserved for those who have both the heart and the faith to yield everything they are, and everything they have, in order to ascend to the heights above. Those who come forth to begin this climb must come empty of self. They come not trusting in their own knowledge and skill, but rather depending, in faith, upon My wisdom to direct every move. When I give the command to proceed upward, they will draw strength from My presence to ascend where it is impossible to do so. When I speak forth a time of rest, these faithful, trusting climbers will drive the nail into the depths of the mountain and find rest being suspended from the support holding up their very lives. Fear will be put behind them as the goal to reach the heights of glory urges them upward.

. Little ones, I long for you to climb to the heights. I yearn to fill your hands with strength and your heart with the fire necessary for the climb. How can I do this if your hands are occupied with worldly things or if your heart is focused upon the things below? You must let go of everything unnecessary for the challenge now placed before you. Your focus must change to embrace My priority and My goal for the climb. I want to teach your eyes to penetrate the darkest night and to pick up the slightest flicker of life in a dying child of mine. You must learn to discern the cracks and the crevices of the mountain, and to see those fragile children who are imprisoned within them. You must come to see from a field of vision and from a perspective of life that is Mine, not yours. I want your mouth to bring forth words that will not only move mountains by faith declared, but to also speak forth proclamations bringing down strongholds at the sounding of My name. I want your ears to perceive the faintest Word of instruction from Me, as well as the faintest whimper of a child, buried under mounds of crushing, entrapping, spiritual rubble. I want your feet to cover miles in a second, as well as to walk upon both water and fire without being dismayed. I want your breath to restore those in suffocation, and your heart to pour out healing love and compassion. These are the traits of those who have climbed to the heights … those who have made a commitment requiring the totality of their being to be surrendered to the call. Are you ready to be remade into a climber of this caliber? I am ready to do this work in you. I have seen your heart of commitment, and I have seen your face turn to embrace the sheer mountain face. I am the One Who has called you to ascend. Your tools are in your hands and My gift of faith upholds you in the climb. There is glory in the heights awaiting you, little ones. There is authority and power being reserved for you to command in My name. You have cried out to me to remake you into one who ascends and into one who occupies the heights. That work is already being done within you, beloved. It is already being done. Breathe in My Spirit and begin to climb.

POWER ...
FOR GOOD OR FOR EVIL

Little ones, there will be times in your life when you feel powerless. I designed you in this way so that you would be aware of your human limitations, lest you begin to think that you are "all powerful." At the same time, I also gave you a significant level of power to apply, so that you might have success in your challenging journey upon the earth. It's very good to know that you have personal power, but it's also important to know how to apply it in a righteous way. You need to know the various forms of human power. Perhaps even more important is that you become aware of the specific applications of your abilities ... which uses of your power will please Me, and which misuses of that power that will displease Me.

It is written that there is no greater power than love. That statement is pure truth. In the present war between My Kingdom and that of the deceiver, this issue of loving others will be looming much larger in the coming days. Therefore, consider with Me: If love is offered generously, purely, faithfully, unconditionally, and genuinely, I am greatly pleased; if, however, your power to impact the heart of another person takes advantage of its strength to punish or to crush someone, by withholding your love, that would be wrong. Using your power of love to manipulate, by making your love for someone conditional until he or she fulfills your demands … until satisfying the terms of love that you have set … is greatly displeasing to Me. You are to reflect My character and My standards when loving. The love that I have for My human children is selfless, upbuilding, sacrificial, patient, and generous. For you to require a person to qualify, in order to receive your love, is a profound contradiction of My character. I love all of My human children— even those who hate Me. Note, however, that I do not love, nor am I obligated to love, all the CHOICES AND BEHAVIORS of My children. I completely love My human creations, without having to love everything that they say or do. You see, I have never stopped loving, but, also, I never started loving, because I AM LOVE. I cannot deny who I AM, nor can I change My reality that has always existed. However, I have given you a choice. You may walk in My way, and reflect, WHO I AM, or you can selfishly, arrogantly, establish terms that satisfy the demands of your flawed character. If you say that you love Me, but then do not love others as I love you, your professions of love for Me are empty words. If you love Me, you will use your love power to love those whom I love. You have Me as your Source and as your teacher in this matter. What more do you need? Do not say that loving is too difficult for you, because pain consumes you. I have given you the POWER to love as I love in the midst of pain. In My most painful hours of torture, My love grew stronger, because love is most vital when pain and rejection are the greatest. It is choosing to love against the flow of hatred and rejection that enables the power of love to defeat death and evil. You simply need to choose to love as I love, and to ask for My love to flow through you to everyone else. If you are battling the obstacles of unhealed wounds, and crippling memories, and find them seizing your heart, come to Me for healing and for deliverance. As you sit in My presence, you will find that My love completely heals and restores, if you allow it. Loving is a choice, which I have enabled within all of My children. Even as you are free to love, you are free to make a choice to withhold love. You may choose to feed love, or allow it to die within your heart. You have the power to choose. You must make your choice to be love, in order to embrace Me. Be aware, however, that to love fully, you must also apply your power to forgive.

Little ones, you know that you have the power to build or to destroy. You have the power to create structures, either according to My inspirations, or according to the input of the enemy. What you build will always bear the signature of the spiritual architect behind it, according to the fruit that is produced. If a structure is raised up to glorify a human being, it will be a planting of evil. It will manifest pride, materialism, control, and unholy power. If a structure prospers life, wholeness, truth, and love, it will be of My design. Use your creative power for building edifices, organizations, and compositions that glorify Me, and which expand My Kingdom. Whatever you build or compose for your own glory and honor, will one day turn into fruitless dust. Whatever you build out of the inspirations of evil, will eventually manifest the fruit of darkness. I, your Creator, desire for you to create things out of the beauty and wisdom that I have inspired within you. Do you not know that I am perpetually creating new things? When you abide with Me in eternity, you will have the delight of participating in that work forever. For now, be careful what you are inspired to create upon the earth. What might seem like an inspired idea, may, in fact, be the blueprint for destruction from My enemy. Ask Me to fill your mind with witty ideas and divine plans. I know exactly what you need to create in order to establish a siege rank against the enemy. Seek My wisdom, and then use your creative power to build that which arises from My inspirations.

Now, consider with Me the power of your tongue. You have a mouth and lips with the ability to produce sound. What is the content of that sound arising from your lips? What is its fruit? Life or death can come into your world through the conduit of your mouth. I have already told you that you have the power to bring forth life through your words. That is what I desire for you. As you speak out of My truth and character, you will bring forth marvelous things, and cause impossible victories to appear. Do you understand that you have the power to drive out darkness with your words? Do you realize that you also have the power to invite darkness to enter into a conflict situation, establishing a legal right for death to abound? Little ones, you are far too careless with your words. You are equally careless in forming the attitudes and assumptions that give rise to your words. You have the power to listen to truth, or to close it out by ignoring it in favor of deception. You have the power to give credibility to suggestions, accusations, and lies, as well as the power to contradict them with the power of spoken truth.

If your heart's priority is set on popularity in the eyes of those around you, very often you will compromise the power you have to align your words with the truth. In those moments, your silence will empower falsehood, supporting the kingdom of darkness. Always use your opportunities to speak in a way that aligns with My Kingdom and with My purposes. In this, I will bless you greatly. To compromise truth, even a little bit, immediately puts you on shaky ground with Me. You may feel as if your silence in a matter of moral truth will put you in a stronger position with the people around you in the world.

However, your compromise will eventually bring evidence of the danger in which you have placed your soul. The enemy has a legal claim to take ground wherever there is rebellion, deceit, pride, and unholy compromise. You cannot be a part-time emissary for Me, and, also, a partial truth-teller. You cannot declare truth and life, and, also, declare words containing death and darkness. You simply cannot speak words of blessing one minute, and then, soon after, spew gossip, slander, and judgment the next, without there being consequences to your security and credibility. Consider which Kingdom will be prospered through each, and all, of your conversations. Check both your words and the heart out of which they speak. You have the power to build or to destroy. You also have the power to influence others to come into My truth, or to continue life apart from Me. Use this vital power very carefully. Be mindful that this power of words is also displayed in whatever you write.

As we consider the issue of human power, I want you to be aware of the material power that I have entrusted to you. Whatever material goods and wealth you have must be used to benefit My purposes. What does it prosper for Me, if you use your wealth to build a comfortable house for yourself, lavishly equipped to impress others? Truly, I have told you to invest in that which is eternal. If you use that house of abundance to extend hospitality to My servants, or to My little ones in need, I will be pleased. If you use it as a place of worship or outreach for the Kingdom, I will be delighted. If you have much material wealth and power, and share much to prosper the work of My Kingdom, you will always receive more substance in return. It is not so much the quantity of items you possess, but whether these things possess the higher priorities of your soul. Those, who have been entrusted with much, have been given these things to share My blessing of abundance with those who I will indicate as the recipients. I will tell you where to invest and where to give. Your job is to ask Me, to hear Me, and to obey Me. You will never out-give Me, but you must not give without consulting Me. Too many give into causes that enable weakness, entitlement, sin, and excuse. That is not pleasing to Me. Look for Kingdom fruit arising from those who are blessed by your giving. Don't look for personal gain. I will tell you where to invest, so that the receivers will come to know Me, and to depend upon Me, because of your generosity, which declares Me. Never give of your material substance for ulterior motives or with the intention of being blessed or honored in return. Those gifts will never be recorded in My Book of Deeds in the High Kingdom. Use your material power wisely. When I say "Store up," then gather up and wait. When I say, "Pour out ... release and distribute," then ask Me where and how much. All things that come from Me are mine. The key in using your material power is to hold things with open hands before Me. Hear My voice and obey Me. You will be blessed; I promise. Be aware that the enemy can also give wealth in abundance. Note the fruit that arises from his "gifts." Many unholy causes and much sin are supported through wrongfully obtained, and wrongfully distributed, wealth and the power that comes with it. Again, behold the source, note the fruit, and be discerning.

Finally, I want to speak to you of physical power and spiritual power. It is possible to move a mountain by using construction equipment. However, that mountain can also be moved by spiritual power in the form of a decree by My dear children, when applied in faith and in obedience to My Word. You most certainly can use your physical power to push back a physical enemy. Likewise, at times, you can push back that same enemy by speaking a word from Me in the Spirit. There are times when I want you to apply your physical power and other times when I want you to exercise your spiritual strength and authority. I will lead you concerning which power to apply in any given circumstance. It will not always be the same in every situation that is similar to another. Listen and discern the anointing that I send for each challenge or task. There will be times when the overwhelming physical threat will prove that physical power is inadequate. I will place you in these threat situations, so that you will give Me great glory by using My Words to speak forth the impossible into earthly reality. Put your faith and your confidence in Me always.

Little ones, it is so important for you to understand that I created you to be powerful, according to My plans for you. You are My warriors, My runners, My overcomers in this fallen world. It does not serve Me for you to demonstrate a false piety based upon weakness, in order to herald your false humility. I want you to live and to operate in the power with which I endowed you ... for My glory. You, also, must know that I created you in a way that will give you even greater power, when you support each other in unity. A chorus of Kingdom voices can shatter the gates of hell, while a single voice can rattle those gates. Come together in the unity of My Spirit and conduct war against the enemy together. Never use any form of your power against each other. Never bully or control others. Never compete or compare yourself against each other. Use your power for Kingdom good, never serving the purposes or character of the enemy.

Now, consider all these things, little ones. Consider carefully and soberly. Put your flesh under submission to My Spirit and resolve to demonstrate My power in the use of your power. Then, arise and live victoriously. Conduct war successfully according to My leading. Love unconditionally. Give generously, according to My instructions. Decree boldly, as you believe and move in absolute faith. Do not fear the enemy but walk in holy awe of the great position of trust in which I have placed you. Know that the power of darkness will never overcome My power, even though, at times, it will appear to be that way. When the enemy thinks he has won, it will be My time to display the depth of My power in you, to utterly humiliate him with defeat. As I have done this in the past, so, also, I will do it in the coming days. Thus, it has been written from ancient times. So, shall it be.

THE FIRES OF HATRED

My heart burns with consuming love for you, little ones. What burns hot within your hearts? What is it that explodes within you? What sets your soul ablaze, giving evidence in your words and actions? Is it love? Is it fear? Is it an ambition to prove yourself in the eyes of others? Is it jealousy? Is it the acquisition of material possessions? Seriously consider My question.

It is My desire for you to be consumed with love for Me and for the things that I love. I want your passions to arise from holiness, not from carnality. I don't want you to set the fervor of your hearts and minds on things that are impermanent and soon to disappear. I want your passions to be ignited by the things that are eternal … upon those things, which will endure forever. I long for the zeal of your heart to advance My Kingdom, and to build, rather than to destroy, that Kingdom. My enemy wants you to operate in contrary priorities and passions.

So much love has been lost between you, little ones. Too many seeds of suspicion, competition, envy, and strife have been planted into the soil of your hearts and minds. Those seeds, planted in receptive soil, have brought forth a harvest of hatred among My children. That, which was the original passion of jealous discontent found in the heart of a fallen angel, was transplanted into My children of the earth. That jealousy took root in the offspring of the first generation, leading to hatred, murder, and death. Love becomes strangled by hatred, which, in turn, strangles the lives of others. Hatred creates a deadly chain reaction, when it is allowed to run its course freely.

Is it comfortable for you to hate, little ones? I have created you for love, and have put within you a heart that is meant to disquiet you whenever you move away from loving. That heart grows and becomes stronger … it beats in perfect rhythm with Me when it is operating with love as its fuel. However, when dark thoughts and dark inclinations of soul move upon a human heart, an alternative fuel presents itself. In that moment, you have a choice in determining what you will allow to empower your disposition. If you choose My love to feed that heart, you will pass through the difficult times and move beyond the temptations of darkness. You will remain in My truth and in My character. If, however, you choose the dark fuel, that is produced from the drippings of deceptions and delusions, to empower your soul, you will abandon My character and My truth to serve an enslaving master. There will always be death and destruction produced by hatred directed against one of My children, or against Me. One of the first things destroyed, when hatred is allowed to burn hot, is the warning alarm set against it that I created within you. When hatred takes root … when it consumes the heart … very soon, the mind will embrace its version of skewed truth. The ears will hear through filters of perverse deception.

You become very vulnerable to these alterations in perceived reality, when My warning mechanisms, which I embedded in your heart, are switched off by pride. Once that total transfer of influence and perception has been accomplished, it will be very difficult for love, or for truth to break through the bondage of this darkness.

I need not tell you about the destruction created by hatred, as it has been demonstrated throughout the generations of human life. The evidence is clear. It continues to be seen, by those who have eyes to see, and heard, by ears willing to hear. But, the thing about hatred is that it quickly becomes wrapped in a spirit of urgency, which demands immediate recruitment and allegiance with the assembly of the hateful. Hate is often introduced swathed in a self-endorsed, seemingly honorable urgency that is embellished by offense, fear, and indignation. If My littles ones draw in close to attend to what offense, fear, and indignation are speaking out of darkness, hatred becomes injected into the soul. Its venom is delivered into the mind and heart, much like the sting of a scorpion, but without the immediate pain. In a strange way, the venom of hatred is found to be comforting. It supports the delusion, and it assures the soul of operating in righteousness indignation and in most certain truth. Hatred claims the moral high ground, when, in fact, it is established in the swampland of the evil one. Be careful, little ones. Do not be deceived into entering that swamp, even if enticed by righteous causes.

Like a malignant virus, hatred can be disseminated though a family line, through a community, or through a population—bringing emotions to a boiling point, while being fueled by lies and delusions that contradict actual reality. Wars arise in this way. Divorces and estrangements evolve, to become viewed as a logical and necessary course, when hatred has arisen into a position of authority within the soul. When hatred is given the high ground, its agenda seeks to crush truth and love. It is written that unity brings strength. Surely, this is true, even when hatred is the basis for unity between people. Unity in truth brings life. Unity established in hatred produces unreasonable horrors, destruction, and death.

Take a close look at your current world, little ones. What do you see? Is it not a spreading devastation fueled by unreasonable hatred? So much of that hatred is based upon delusions. So much more is founded upon pride that has been infested with jealousy. My enemy has sent forth his emissaries with goads in their hands. They prod the souls of My children with skewed words and with false perceptions that wound, threaten, and offend them. They inject blame and judgment into these places of abrasion until a major infection sets in. Unless this stream is intentionally rejected, very soon, the thoughts and emotions of judgment and condemnation will take a place of predominance in the heart and mind. The inflow of negativity will continue until hatred is so well established that ignoring its call becomes nearly impossible. At that point, hatred begins to burn hot. The memories of blessings, benefits, and historical truth turn to ash in the blaze. The agenda of the soul is then set into place according to the demands of hatred. That agenda is intended to spread hatred from one person to another, until a unified voice will declare the lies as truth ... until the demand for justice arises in power to intimidate and to crush the voices of truth. Sadly, My truth-tellers are reticent to speak forth in unity, because of the threats leveled against their perspectives. The silent truth-tellers see the fire and feel the heat of it. Many will step back in the hope that the fires of hatred might soon burn out. However, these little ones fail to understand that there is MUCH available fuel within the human environment ... enough to keep these unholy fires burning until the end of time.

So, what are you to do about these fires of hatred? Give them no fuel from your own soul. Accept no spark or burning ember from another person. Prepare yourself to walk among the flames. How is this done? Be perpetually saturated in living water flowing from My Spirit. Stay in My Word of truth, and formulate your reality based upon My actuality. Establish your perceptions and your conclusions according to My input. Wear the armor that I have provided for you, so that the goading and the lethal injections from My enemy will have no effective way to impact your soul. Choose to love. Choose to remember the good things, and the certain things, based upon My love and reality in your life. Extend grace to those, who offend your soul. Forgive freely. Other people WILL hurt you with their words and actions, often unintentionally. If the intention is to harm or to disqualify you, your attackers may spew condemnation and rejection solely because of your positions and beliefs, which they find to be objectionably contrary to theirs. Stand your ground, and do not lower your position by returning similar fire toward them. You do not have to gain their agreement, nor their affection. Simply continue to speak wisely, love faithfully, and stand humbly. Trust Me to be with you in the fires of hatred being leveled against you. Keep your eyes upon Me, and keep walking ahead. Do not be silent with the truth, but be sure to speak it forth boldly, consistently, and clearly, in love, while standing upon My foundations, abiding in My shalom.

Soon, the whole world will be in a state of spiritual battle to a level unseen before. The spiritual war will manifest daily in very tangible, and often painful, ways. Endure! Through the example of My three servants, who once stood in the overwhelming heat of a fiery furnace, refusing to surrender the truth, unwilling to bow in the face of threating death, I have shown you the way you are to go. Even as I was with these three, faithful truth-tellers in the intense blaze, I will be with you in your times of trial as well. These unfolding days will present you with many challenges and tests of faith. Do not fear. Even now, stablish a commitment in your heart to lovingly hold firmly on behalf of those issues that are essential in My Kingdom. Discipline your mind to focus upon My truth alone. Open your eyes to see what I am doing in the midst of difficulty and threat. When the fires of hatred seek to consume you, a blessed mystery will appear. In the intense heat, I will be refining pure gold within you. All that is not of Me will be burned away, so that the value of your life will increase greatly in Kingdom treasure.

The enemy and his servants will hate you. They will pursue you relentlessly. They will attack the people you love the most in an effort to burn away your faith and to transfer hatred into your soul. Do not yield, nor be deceived. Take your stand with love and endure on that high ground. Wherever there is no fuel to be burned, the fires of hatred have no real power. Your body may perish in the blaze, if it is My time to bring you home. You will not have been defeated, but, rather, will have been victorious, if that is My chosen course for you. However, if My plan is for you to continue presenting opposition to the evil of this world, rejoice. I will accomplish much through your love and faith. Your suffering will produce an authority that will enable you to walk with the fire under your feet. That faithful endurance will grant you the ability to speak directly to the fire, causing it to turn away or to be quenched on the spot. Allow My plan for your life to unfold, in My way and in My timing. Trust Me. Come together! Assemble in unity with all of My children of truth and faithfulness. Be of one voice and of one mind … MINE! Those who have made hatred the substance of their garments and the cause of their lives, will continue to increase on the earth. Do not be intimidated. Do not become frustrated when your heart, words, and actions are condemned, misrepresented, and decried by the masses. Do not give up, when your efforts seem to have no impact upon their destructive course or perspectives. I will deal with the deceptive and with the deluded. Just keep walking forward, fulfilling your Kingdom call. In the fullness of time, all that resists My authority … all that has countered My Kingdom … will be consumed in My holy fire. That fire will not be quenched throughout all eternity. Until then, I want you to burn with holy fire, fueled by My love. Allow My light to shine through you into this great darkness. You will bring forth life when the world is rushing toward death. You will be used to snatch many from the power of unholy fires, as I burn within you. Be one with Me. In this way, your life will be fulfilled. My Kingdom WILL come with all its glory. You will see it, because you will be there with Me in the midst of it.

CONCUDING COMMENTS
FROM THE SCRIBE OF
THE CRY *of the* SHEPHERD

If you would ask me, "What did you learn most from receiving and recording this book?" I would have to say that it has shown me the victorious side of surrendered brokenness. To approach matters of spiritual warfare having the sense that we know much of anything, let alone everything about it, makes us vulnerable to defeat. Certainly, we know that the Messiah has accomplished our ultimate victory, but how we experience that victory in our daily warfare is another matter. Truly, we MUST work out our salvation in fear and trembling, lest we assume that we know precisely the specifics through which the Shepherd will be manifesting His victory, in each encounter we have with the enemy. The Shepherd's way of warfare breaks all the carnal rules of engagement. His strategies sometimes defy our human understanding, and, at times, they even offend our souls. For a Shepherd to war against the powers of hell by becoming a shorn, silent, and sacrificed lamb makes no sense to us. That is not how we battle our enemies. We prefer the conventional means of hand-to-hand combat, applying emotional and mental force, until we overpower those who challenge us or who discredit us. We prefer a battle of wits to take place in front of witnesses, so that we can be publicly seen as righteously victorious, vindicated, and right. We often believe that we have an effective supply of human power to wield against attackers and, therefore, do not hesitate to apply it. As a result, our battles are more intense and more costly. Our losses are greater, and our witness is dimmed. We have been told that we do not war against flesh and blood, and yet every day we fight using those carnal weapons in battles with each other … in battles empowered and inspired by dark spiritual forces, aligned to defeat us. People continually come into our line of fire, and they repeatedly become the targets of our warfare. Meanwhile, the influence of our own selfish, jealous, and prideful flesh is ignored. So often, our flesh calls us to battle and it eagerly supplies the weapons. So often, we label both our struggle and our strategies as holy war.

The Shepherd's methods in war are always in agreement with the Shepherd's character at all times. He does not battle unholiness with unholiness, but rather with holiness. He does not battle offense by self-defending, but by demonstrating a righteousness that shows his enemies to be liars concerning Him. He makes war against pride by presenting humility. He releases captives by allowing Himself to temporarily be taken captive. Who can understand such things? When assaulted, He forgives before there is any admission of fault from the other. His character is mercy.

Sadly, there are portions of the flock that see these characteristics of the Shepherd as being merciful to sin and to evil, so they, too, extend tolerance toward sin, allowing it to overpower them and others. This is an absolutely false interpretation of His character. He is violent against wickedness in the time of His chosen judgment. He is incessantly filled with zeal against wicked powers. However, to our great benefit, He is able to look at us with eyes unlike our own. He sees the reality of His dream created in us, when it has been erased by sin from our exterior beings, from our actions, and from our words. In great love, He cries out to that dream … to that creation at our beginning ... calling it from within us to arise and to come forth. Mercy and love are His character; therefore, He calls us to be merciful and loving with each other, but never with the evil forces that assail others and us. The distinction is critically important, but it is often misunderstood. Even the power of His Word of truth is a cutting weapon, which must be applied with a love and mercy that is not natural to our own flesh. He must be the one to command us. He must be the model we follow. His eyes must become ours in order for us to see the battle and the enemy clearly enough to strike the blows.

There are times when it seems as if we have been utterly defeated while using His commanded weapons and strategies. This is never the case. Even if it seems as if the opposition has had the upper hand and left us in defeat, if we have not veered from His character, we have won. The manifestation of that victory is simply yet to be seen. One day we may discover that we have a change of heart, not realizing that it is the product of the completed, victorious warfare. A time may come when a person, once a virulent enemy, comes to us in a new spirit and heart. Because of the hot coals rained down upon his or her head by the mercy of God as a result of our completed warfare, we now have an ally. Perhaps we will not see the victory until we have reached eternity. Even without visible evidence, we must know that the way of the Shepherd in warfare, and in all matters concerning our lives, is victory.

The words of this book have opened my eyes as He spoke them into my spirit. I now see many of the repeated assaults and the familiar attacks as precious opportunities. They have been a way in which I have been trained and tested. They have offered me the opportunities to experience the pain and the futility of human weapons against human flesh and demonic powers. Many years ago, He told me that I would feel the sting of human blindness and experience the injustice and imprisonment of these things prospered against my life as a result. At the same time, when I was given this announcement of warning in the Spirit, He also told me that as I endured and walked the painful experiences with Him … in the manner of His heart … I would emerge with much greater authority. In time, the enemies would be silenced by <u>Him</u>.

Reflecting back upon my life, I can see where I have failed to respond out of His character when attacked. I can see the carnal weapons and the carnal inclinations that quickly fell into my hands and wounded heart. I can also see how ineffective they were in changing anything in the battle, except to prolong it and to intensify it. The Shepherd has been abundantly merciful in giving me evidence of the victory when I have followed His lead, engaging the proper enemy in the ordained way … when I have died to flesh rather than use it to battle the flesh of another person. Do I have more to learn? Do I require more practice to become more skilled? Absolutely! The Cry of the Shepherd has again confirmed the way for me to go. The teachings have clarified the realities and the challenges of the war that surrounds us. It has reminded me of the glory awaiting the Kingdom as I fight for His causes with His weapons. Isn't that what it's all about … HIS GLORY? If my glory ever becomes a consideration, I am defeated by the enemy and by my own flesh in the first moment of battle. Even when the enemy corners me, and when I have lost ground for having left the battle plan, the good news is that the Shepherd stands near, continually calling out the change of strategy and offering the correct weapons. I only need to heed His cry and obey Him to emerge victorious.

God bless you, as you, too, experience the challenges of spiritual war and in your battles against human flesh. I pray that in the final day of victory, I will look through the ranks, as one of the victorious redeemed, to find you standing there with me. Until then, may we all battle righteously, faithfully, skillfully, courageously, and obediently. May we all fight the true enemy. May we set many captives free and give grace to all of the flock, who stand with us in battle. And, in all things, may we reflect our Shepherd's character … the greatest manifestation of which is love. No one has greater love than the Shepherd, who laid down His life for His little flock. May we do the same.

ADDITIONAL RESOURCES

PROTOCOLS FOR PRAYER WARRIORS

Morning Prayer

Father God, Yehovah, I plead the covering of the shed blood of Yeshua Ha Mashiach (Jesus the Messiah/ the Christ) over all of us, Your children. I pray for Your protection, Your blessing, Your provision, Your revelation, Your holiness, and Your wisdom to be upon us. Saturate each one of us with these endowments, transforming all, who have been created by You, into living testimonies of Your glory.

I pray for salvation and for deliverance to come, and to apprehend all the members of my household who are not saved … and all those not walking in the salvation they once accepted. I pray the same grace and mercy to be upon all those who You have placed upon my heart and upon my prayer lists. Intercept, apprehend, and turn around all those, who are not saved, as well as those saved, but who are now backslidden, and no longer operating as the redeemed of the Lord. Destroy the false grids that keep the minds and hearts of Your children locked in deception. Cause truth to finally dissolve whatever has been walling out Your love and revelations. Set the captives free to <u>truly</u> know You. Please, hem them in, using whatever means is necessary, so that they will not be lost to You, even if that means they may be estranged from us in this life.

I pray for Your loving intervention to be upon all those who are stumbling. Intervene for those who are blind and being attacked or controlled by doubts, pride, witchcraft, rage, deceptions, skepticism, jealousy, lust, and fear. Open the blind eyes; remove the veil. Unstop the deaf ears and remove the demonic filters. Warm up the cold hearts and heal the wounds that have put these manifestations of rejection into place. Help them to see Your love and truth, which is their only source of real freedom and wholeness. In mercy, cause all idolatry to utterly fail, all delusions to be exposed as false reality, and all strongholds to utterly shatter, so that the deceived may find You as their Sovereign Lord.

Enable us to love <u>AS</u> You love, and help us to love <u>WHAT</u> You love, while standing back from endorsing, tolerating, enabling, or embracing whatever You hate. Cause Your love to lead and to govern us in all things. Give us the ability to know the difference between what Your definition of the word LOVE means, over and above what the world system declares it to be. Empower us to always choose Your love, and then to demonstrate it faithfully. Help us to do this even if the cost of our faithfulness to Your way, will, and Word becomes the world's rejection and disdain for us. Enable us to be courageous, and lovingly faithful to You, unto death, regardless of the level of opposition, and the severity of threatened losses.

I pray for the healing, which was bought for us by the wounds from Yeshua's flogging, to manifest today in miraculous ways. Cause that healing and deliverance to come forth in the bodies, minds, and emotions, of all those who are sick, damaged, oppressed, possessed, or afflicted in any way. Give us many opportunities to testify of Your healing power. Grant us miracles when they are needed, and manifest them in such a way that no one, except for You, will receive the glory.

Lord I pray for Your hand to be upon each and every one of us, for Kingdom gain, granting that we would exhibit Your character while engaging with each of the contacts and relationships you have provided for us. Enable us to demonstrate Your manner of heart, help, grace, and wholeness in all that we think, say, or do throughout this day.

Help us to discern those individuals who have come into our lives, or who are about to cross our paths, that are sent by the enemy and not by You. Forbid that we would be deceived by taking into our hearts, or homes, anyone who would give the enemy an opportunity to have access to us for loss, deception, or destruction. Protect us from absorbing any element of falsehood into our thinking, into our choices of behavior, or into our emotions. Lock us down in Your truth alone.

I pray that You would be before us, behind us, above us, below us, beside us, and all about us every moment. I pray that as You organize this day, You would sovereignly take us, or direct us, from one divine appointment to another … from one "Kingdom" conversation to another. Help us to recognize these ordained opportunities, so that we would avail ourselves to accomplish whatever it is that You desire for us. Feel free to redirect our planned course today, if an unexpected, "divine interruption" involving our clock and calendar is part of Your plan.

I pray for Your hand to be upon all of our means of transportation and provision required throughout this day. I pray for safe travelling mercies for each one of us and for all of those who may be travelling with us and around us. Send forth Your appointed angels to accompany us throughout this day, undertaking on our behalf as You have instructed them to do. We welcome their help.

Regarding any machines or electronic devices that we may operate ... or that others may operate, impacting our lives in any way ... please prosper them to function for our good, for our safety, and for Your glory. Protect us from any harmful electronic waves, energies, vapors, or particulates, and shield us from all manner of mind control and evil manipulation.

Please protect us from all threats that would come against us from any direction, in any form, at any time. Also, please protect us from our sinful selves, wherever and whenever needed, throughout this day. Especially rescue us from our own arrogance, presumption, and foolishness, which could possibly manifest in our speaking or behaviors. Help us to avoid creating unnecessary pain and problems for ourselves, and for others, through errors arising from our soul ... those ugly, negative, demonstrations of our undisciplined, wounded, prideful, or deceived flesh, which would sully Your reputation. Give us humble discernment, and reveal to us every snare, bait, and trap of the enemy, so that we might avoid being seduced, entangled, distracted, delayed, or deceived in any way. Forbid that we would extend unsanctified, soulish mercy toward any person or situation where You have not chosen to extend mercy, in order to prosper a higher purpose beyond our understanding. Forbid that we would enable sin and rebellion to thrive in any form. Please cover the vulnerable places in our soul, and teach us to defend whatever You desire to endure and to grow, within us or within others.

Father, make us wise, loving, patient, bold, faithful, and perceptive. Cause us to reflect Your heart and mind in all circumstances. Where we lack grace for those around us, please give us an anointing of divine grace. Give us ears to hear Your assessments of situations and give us eyes to see Your unfolding plans at work. Give us hearts that are teachable and willing to follow in faith wherever You lead us throughout this day. Guide us solely and sovereignly by Your truth, causing us to know it, to speak it, and to live it, without compromise. Anoint us with divine holiness, humility, submission, obedience, and love.

Father, cause us, by Your Spirit, to seek unity, and to be locked together in that holy unity, established in Your truth, and shalom, rather than being perpetrators of unholy division. Father God, rebuke Leviathan and send him away. Make us ONE in You. Shelter us, as individuals and as a Body, under Your wings, so that we will find our rest in You.

Bless all of Your children and all of Your creatures, so that ALL of Your creation may bring You great glory this day, accomplishing Your perfect will in all things. B'shem Yeshua Ha Mashiach (in the name of Jesus the Messiah)! AMEN!

Putting on the armor of YHVH

Father, I ask that You would cover me in the blood of Yeshua Ha Mashiach from the top of my head to the soles of my feet and to the tips of my fingers … spirit, soul, and body.

I place, upon my entire being, the whole armor which You have provided.

On my head, I place the Helmet of Salvation … with the visor down, so that the enemy will not see my face, but that I will see and discern his every move made against me or against those I love.

On my chest, I place the Breastplate of Righteousness (from

213

Yeshua's priesthood), which covers my heart, and establishes the loving servant heart of the Messiah within me.

Around my waist, I place the Belt of Truth to keep me from error and from all unholy compromise. This truth protects my emotions and inspires my words and actions according to Your Eternal Truth and wisdom, helping me to be established in, and to operate with, the courage and conviction necessary for taking a righteous stand for Your Kingdom … and for conducting successful spiritual warfare whenever it is required.

On my feet and legs, I place the Shoes of Readiness to present the Gospel of Peace. Bless these shoes to protect me from the bite of the viper and from the sting of the scorpion, as they carry me from one "seeker" to another … and from one divine appointment to another. Make me sure-footed. Cause these shoes to keep me balanced, on the right path, and protected from stumbling.

In my right hand, I pick up and carry with me the Sword of the Spirit, which is Your Word, Mighty YHVH. I pray for wisdom and discernment in its use and application, so that the lies of the enemy would be utterly cut down … so that those bound in deception would be set free.

On my left arm and hand, I carry the Shield of Faith. It protects me from slander, lies, delusions, witchcraft, fear, and all other attacks of the enemy, through which he would seek to make me doubtful, hesitant, intimidated, or unfaithful to the obedience of Your Truth. Never allow these incoming attacks to cause me to abandon the course or the calling, which You have entrusted to me.

In addition, I ask for the tools to minister healing, strength, restoration, and freedom. Fill me with Your Holy Spirit. Mark me with the blood of Yeshua the Messiah, and entrust to me a pouch to hang from my belt, carrying that which has been infused with Your Presence by the Holy Spirit ... a flask of Living Water, and a vial of the oil of holy anointing, to bring strength and restoration to the sick, to the wounded, to the broken, to the bound, to the perishing, to the weakened, to the blinded, and to the discouraged. Let these gifts and graces from You, entrusted to me, humbly manifest Your Kingdom's authority and power throughout this day. Give me the faith, the discernment, and the courage to apply the spiritual gifts in obedience to the leading of Your Spirit.

Fill me now with Your divine breath, as I inhale Your love. As I exhale, I release my life and this day into Your hands. SECURE ME, SEAL ME, and SEND ME, Lord. This day is YOURS, even as I AM YOURS! B'shem Yeshua HaMashiach, AMEN.

Bedtime Prayer

Father God, Yehovah, as I settle down to sleep, I entrust my entire being into Your hands. Blind my eyes, deafen my ears, and seal me ... spirit, soul, and body ... with the blood of Yeshua the Messiah. As I sleep, forbid that I would receive any input into my being other than the input that You would give to me. Please place a platform of holy fire underneath my house and property, and a canopy of holy fire over it. Set up a wall of fire all around this house and property. Sanctify this set apart space, driving from it anything that is not of You. Purify the air I breath and enable my body to be renewed in this sanctified environment as I sleep. Forbid that there would be any astral projection or soul travel into or through this property by human spirits, by spirits of the dead, by demonic spirits, or by fallen angels. Lock out any access to me, to my loved ones, or to this property that might be sought by those practicing the magic arts and satanic rituals. Send Your holy angels to protect me and to minister to me, as needed, while I rest in the palm of Your hand this night. Prepare me, during this time of rest, so that I will be better equipped to meet the challenges that will come in the hours and days ahead. I invite Your revelations to come into my dreams. Cause me to remember and to understand the dreams You send, blowing away any thought that comes to me in the night that is not of You. My waking hours are Yours and so are my hours of sleep. I surrender to Your sovereignty, and trust in Your divine cover. Use these hours of my sleep for Your divine purposes, however You choose. I worship you and bless You for all that You are, and I thank You for all that You give. All honor, glory, dominion, and power are Yours alone. B'shem Yeshua Ha Mashiach, AMEN.

Steps To Set Aside And Secure Your Home And Property For Kingdom Use

Why Do This?

For those of you who are feeling the call of the Lord to secure your property, setting it aside for Kingdom purposes in the days ahead, here is a format that you may apply. As always, seek the Lord for confirmation before taking these steps.

You will first anoint and pray through the buildings (your home, office building, etc.). When that is finished, you will walk around the borders of your property seven times carrying Kosher salt and olive oil (depositing a bit of salt at the four corners of your property boundaries and sprinkling droplets of olive oil on the ground as you walk). There will be seven specific areas of declaration and decree; one area of focus for each of the seven rounds you make. Why the salt and oil? The

216

salt is a sign of making a covenant with the Lord, as well as being part of the offering (the flavor) you make of your property for His service.

> *"Every grain offering of yours, moreover, you shall season with salt, so that the salt of the covenant of your God shall not be lacking from your grain offering; with all your offerings you shall offer salt"*
> Leviticus 2:13

The olive oil is for sanctification … setting the property apart as something holy to the YHVH. Whatever the Lord possesses, He defends and fortifies. Olive oil was historically used to anoint the land/buildings for holy use, establishing a holy barrier/boundary, and to bring it under holy protection. Both the salt and oil are symbols of healing and restoration as well. Whatever has been depleted or harmed, we ask be restored.

Summarizing the process then: The property is being set aside for the purposes of the Lord … sanctified, set-apart. Through this act you are making a covenant and delineating your property as an offering to being made to the Lord for His use. During this time that you are marking your property and land; setting it aside for the Lord according to its boundaries of ownership. You will also be breaking any unholy claims and curses made upon the land or property. These open doorways, granting legal access for evil, may have been established by your own sin or unholy contracts, or by these things in the history of the property, committed by other people, not by you.

Additionally, you will be cursing, ejecting, and forbidding (by the hand, word, and decree of YHVH) anything ungodly that might try to remain, or to enter into/onto the property in the future. As you walk, pray, and declare the scriptures, the Lord will be tearing up the deeds of access and evicting any evil trespassers. As you repent for your own sin and ask the Lord to cover the sin (which is on the land and property) even that which preceded your ownership, the land becomes secured, cleansed, and refreshed.

NOTE: In this intense spiritual environment and era of heavy witchcraft, it's often good to do this annually at the time of a New Year. It's a reminder to ourselves, and to the dark powers, that we are still committed and serious in our service to YHVH. We look to HIM alone to be all that we need. He is our defense. We will not be moved. By His grace and by His enabling, we shall stand, speak, and live for HIM.

STEP #1
Prepare For Cleansing And Dedicating
The Building And Land

Begin by setting yourselves apart. Sit with the Lord and quietly confess what the Holy Spirit shows you is sin in need of being recognized, repented, and covered by the atonement of the Messiah. This is an act of humility and dedication. Then partake of unleavened bread and wine (or grape juice) in remembrance, and in acknowledgement, of the Passover sacrifice made by the broken body and shed blood of Yeshua the Messiah (Jesus the Christ). He is the Redeemer of all humanity. He is the Redeemer of our days and of our property. Have a small bottle of anointing oil in hand or take a small bottle of pure olive oil, and pray for it to be sanctified by the Holy Spirit … set apart for holy use. (You will not use that bottle of oil for any other purpose in the future)

> *[If] My people who are called by My name humble themselves and pray and seek My face and turn from their wicked ways, then I will hear from heaven, will forgive their sin and will heal their land*
> *(2 Chronicles 7:14).*

218

Consecrate yourselves, therefore, and be holy, for I
am the LORD your God (Leviticus 20:7)

PROCEED with STEP #2:
Blessing The House
(or other building such as an office)

Begin the protocol on the ground floor, at the center point of the building. Touch the floor with a drop of oil and declare that this house belongs to the Lord, and that those, who dwell in the house will give Him praise. Invite the Holy Spirit to come fill the house. Ask the Lord to send His appointed angels to escort out everything that is unholy, as your prayers and decrees are made.

Now, go to the **basement**, if you have one. (If you don't have a basement, go to the protocol for the second floor. If you don't have a second floor, proceed with the protocol for the main floor.) Put your hand with a drop of oil on the floor at the center of the room. Ask the Lord to sanctify with the blood of the Messiah, the ground underneath the building, the rock, the water, and the substances of earth as far down as it goes … throughout all of history. In the name, blood, and authority of Yeshua the Messiah, cancel all unholy covenants, spilled blood, and spiritual contracts made against the land; blotting out all sin embedded in the ground. Then touch each of the four walls with oil, and each mechanical/electrical device, water source and drain … sealing them in the blood of the Messiah. Anoint the bottom of the stairs, and pray as you go up the stairs, asking the Lord to forbid any tripping, falling, or accident from taking place on them (in the name, blood, and authority of Yeshua the Messiah, Jesus the Christ). At the top, anoint the top step, and the two side posts of the door frame, as well as the frame over the door.

Now, go to the **second floor** if you have one (go to the protocol for the main floor if you have a one level dwelling.) Walk up the stairway and go into each room … touching the center point floor of each room with oil, and then touching each wall, window frame, bed head, mirror, and electric device (TV for example), and air vent. As you exit the room, anoint the door from the top frame to the threshold, then each side frame. Do this for each room. In the bathroom, also anoint the drains and water sources, as well as the air vents. As you exit, anoint the frame as noted above. When you have finished anointing all the rooms and are preparing to go down the stairs, ask the Lord to sanctify the air throughout the house, and the air and space over and around it. Ask Him to sanctify and secure all the structures of the house, and all its contents. Anoint the top step, and as you go down the stairs, ask the Lord to forbid any tripping, falling, or accident from taking place on them (in the name, blood, and authority of Yeshua the Messiah … Jesus the Christ).

Now, you should be back on the **ground level floor**. If you have an attached garage, go there and anoint the walls and the doors, asking the Lord to seal and secure them under the blood of Yeshua the Messiah. Then go to each of the rooms on this level. Mark the walls with a drop of oil, as well as the center point of each room, and each window. Touch each electric appliance, electronic device, and air vent sealing them, and securing them under the authority of the Messiah. As you exit each room that has a door, anoint the door from the top frame, then down to the floor, then each side frame. If you have a back door, anoint the threshold and frames as above. If you have a fireplace, anoint around it as well, and pray for protection against any fire that would try to escape from the fire chamber, and any misplaced fire that would occur within the chimney.

At this point you should have the whole house anointed. Now stand at the front door and open it. Stand in the doorway and ask the Lord to sweep everything unholy from the house at this time. Again, decree and declare that this house will stand and serve the purposes of the Lord YHVH. Then, exit the house and anoint the frame above the door, the threshold, and then the two side frames. If there are steps up into the house, anoint them and pray for the Lord to allow into the house, only those who the Lord approves. Pray for protection against accidents and stumbling on those steps. Ask the Lord to post His angels to stand guard at the entrance of the house. Ask for Him to post angels on all sides, at the back entrance, and on the roof. The house is now blessed and sealed.

PROCEED WITH STEP #3
Setting Aside The Grounds And
Marking The Borders/Boundaries:

Begin at your front door, making the declaration that recognize YHVH's Lordship over your life, your home, and over the property, declaring that the property was entrusted to you on behalf of His Kingdom. Ask the Lord to protect what is His, and to enable you to be good stewards of His trust. Gather some kosher salt and carry it with you, along with the sanctified olive oil

Walk around the very edges of your property line, pausing at each of the four corners briefly with each round, to state the declaration of each particular round. Sprinkle a bit of Kosher salt at the corners (each time you come to one) and occasionally drop oil on your path each time around.

Speak out this scripture:

> He went out to the spring of water and threw salt
> in it and said, "Thus says the LORD, 'I have purified

221

these waters; there shall not be from there death or unfruitfulness any longer" (2 Kings 2:21).

Here is the declaration you speak forth:

We declare and claim the protection of the Lord YHVH, by His hand, and supported by His angels for each of the issues mentioned for each trip around this property. In addition, we ask the Lord to cleanse the land itself of all sin and iniquity, with the blood of Yeshua the Messiah, down to the deepest level … cancelling all previous unholy covenants, spilled blood, and unholy claims.

Ask Him to sever all ley lines into and through the property, establishing this ground as holy unto Him.

As you begin each round, speak out what is being canceled and what the property is being protected from, as listed below. Cancel these things in the name, blood, and authority of Yeshua the Messiah (Jesus the Christ). Focus your prayers specifically on the designated issues for each trip around. Speak protection against these things and offer thanksgiving to the Lord for bringing His protection. Pray in the Spirit as the Lord leads, and speak out any scriptures that He may give to you for each round. Sing and worship as you go, as led by the Spirit.

1. The first time around the property pray for protection against the shaking, splitting, sinking, or spewing earth (earthquake, volcano, sinkhole. etc.).

2. The second time, protection against swirling wind, straight-line wind, or down-draft.

3. The third time, protection against flooding, water and ice.

4. The fourth time, protection against fire, lightening, and any blast (nuclear, EMP, etc.).

5. The fifth time, protection against theft or break[in?] invasion by any human or inhuman enemy and a[ny] kidnapping and murder.

6. The sixth time, protection against plague, pestilence, [poi?] sonous vapors, harmful energy waves, and toxic eleme[nts] from the sky or from the ground.

7. The seventh time, protection against any impact from fal[l?] ing or crashing objects (meteors, bombs, asteroids, falling planes, falling trees, rockets, etc.) … as well as any access by evil cosmic beings (including any/all beings of the Dark Kingdom, whether occultic, satanic, demonic, spirits of the dead or human spirits … whether by astral projection, by soul travel, or by the use of ley lines or other sorcery.

When you have completed all seven times around the property, with each focus addressed, ask the Lord to post angels at the four corners of the property boundaries, and at the entrance of the driveway onto the property.

Again, go to the front door and anoint the threshold, doorframe, and lintels with the sanctified olive oil. Ask the Lord to fill you (and everyone who lives in the house), as well as the property, with His light, and enable you to take that light out from there into the neighborhood and beyond. Ask the Lord to make your home a place of sanctuary where people will find safe hospitality, healing, deliverance, truth, salvation, love, and restoration (seven things). In a final gesture blow a shofar, if you have one, and raise a shout of praise to the Lord. If you don't have a shofar, ask the Lord to have one blown in the High Kingdom for you as you give Him praise on the earth.

in, and
gainst

poi-
nts

l-

To purchase more copies, for information on
distribution, or to view all products available through
DEEPER REVELATION BOOKS

Visit our website:
www.deeperrevelationbooks.org
Phone: 423-478-2843

Mailing address:
P. O. Box 4260
Cleveland, TN 37320